ARE WE FORGETTING SOMETHING?

edited by
HARRY BOHAN
and
GERARD KENNEDY

VERITAS

First published 1999 by
Veritas Publications
7/8 Lower Abbey Street
Dublin 1

Copyright © The individual contributors 1999

ISBN 1 85390 457 0

British Library Cataloguing
in Publication Data.
A catalogue record for
this book is available
from the British Library.

Cover design by Bill Bolger
Printed in the Republic of Ireland by Betaprint Ltd, Dublin

CONTENTS

PART THREE: EXPERIENCE OF AUTHORITY –
AUTHORITY OF EXPERIENCE

FOREWORD

Harry Bohan

Irish Society is experiencing dramatic change. The country is in the middle of a period of unprecedented economic growth, bringing with it a welcome increase in prosperity and material well-being. Although the impact of growth is not spread among areas or social groups, it is nonetheless welcome and long overdue. Our society is long familiar with the costs of economic failure. Emigration, the breakdown of peripheral communities, poverty, and unemployment were the public manifestation of failure. For the first time in our short history as an independent country, we are free to make some real choices.

However, even in the short period of the 'Celtic Tiger' it is becoming increasingly obvious that Irish society, as distinct from the economy, is beginning to pay a high and unacceptable price for the material prosperity.

Ireland is now part of a global economic system and we are fast becoming an affluent society. The country in all its dimensions is increasingly shaped by the needs and agenda of the corporate world. Big corporations are now the engines which drive most aspects of political, social and economic life, and which permeate the individual at the level, in particular, of consumer needs.

It is universally accepted that the recent growth is founded on the education and newly-developed skills and aptitudes of Irish people. Therefore it is ironic that current development is being increasingly shaped by the remote large corporation with economic criteria the main and sometimes sole arbiter of change. People, place, roots, and, dare we say, soul, are secondary considerations in the decision-making process and often totally ignored in our headlong rush to economic nirvana.

So, are we forgetting something?

At RRD's November 1998 Conference, a cross-section of Irish society came together for three days to pose questions and to search for some answers.

The Conference set out to address questions such as the human search for meaning, managing our future, who are the 'losers' in times of economic boom, sense of place, the media and our vision for the new millennium, the global economy, the power of voluntarism and the importance of community. They concluded that balance and integration – soul/body, local/global – must be restored to our society in the next millennium.

Four main issues emerged as needing urgent attention as we move towards the third millennium:

1. Understanding the nature of change;

2. Re-awakening the inner dimension of our lives;

3. Understanding the influence of the global economy and media;

4. The rediscovery of the local – people, place, belonging, community, spirituality, roots.

Understanding change

Professor John Drew of Durham University's Institute for the Study of Change in Society told us that 'the millennium is a time of great opportunity for our planet. It is also a time of considerable danger. A new year gives cause for reflection, a hundred years even more so. A millennium is something altogether different, especially as it falls by chance, in the middle of three or four decades of the most profound changes our planet has ever witnessed'. For example, it is simply amazing that governments are failing to assess the implications of the move from 1999 to 2000 by computer clocks.

According to Professor Drew, the optimistic aspects of the millennium are to do with new beginnings, with an opportunity to examine the influence on human beings of the global, what is happening to the environment; issues influencing a society which wants and needs to live and work in small units, reaching back emotionally to villages and small towns. But the greatest change of all may come from the fact that we have been exploring our outer world during the second millennium. The indications are that the emphasis in the third millennium may be to work on the re-awakening of the inner dimension of our lives. So a major challenge to our society is to try to understand change if we have any chance of managing it and our future. Professor Drew told us that 'after hundreds of thousands of years as hunter-gatherers in a civilisation whose structure was tribal, we spent only three thousand years in an agrarian civilisation whose society was feudal. The Industrial Revolution saw the development of the nation state and an industrial civilisation, which lasted for only a few hundred years. Now we find ourselves hurtling in a few decades and at an ever-increasing pace, into an information, communications and technology based civilisation.'

Just as our economic and societal arrangements are changing, we are developing rapidly as individuals. We demand freedom. Since the fall of communism a deluge of relativism has gripped us. There are no absolutes. This problem needs to be confronted. What is truth? Pilate asked this question and he washed his hands of responsibility for his actions. In posing this question, our society, like Pilate, is reflecting that we may no longer know who we are, whence we came and where we are going. Are we witnessing the plunging of the human person into situations of gradual self-destruction? The claim to total freedom, the unenlightened conscience (mind) is leading to serious devaluing of human life. The Truth of God is the overture of the Truth of Man. It is vital for our society to understand the kind of change which is taking place if a response is to be found.

There are also changes taking place in the world of business, with corporations here today and gone tomorrow, in the external environment and in civilisation.

The question is – How can we respond to these challenges? We need to widen and deepen the debate, try to understand change. This would go some way towards managing that part of our future we can influence.

The inner dimension of our lives:

Our role models – the family, the Church, the State and others are experiencing the wind of change in a big way. They have weakened as sources of authority. But this vacuum is being filled by the rebirth of a personal, sometimes spiritual dimension in our lives. It is unco-ordinated at this stage but it does present a challenge as to how this concern with the breakdown of relationships leading to a need for community and the development of the inner self can be responded to.

A number of speakers underlined the importance of developing the inner side of life, of nourishing the soul and honestly acknowledging the human condition – its dark and its light. Carl Jung was quoted: 'Your vision will become clear only when you can look into your heart; who looks outside, dreams, who looks inside, awakes.' The contemplative dimension of our lives should be the place where we find our God. If we neglect it we break our relationship with him.

But if a hallmark of society in the third millennium is to search for a soul we must first acknowledge our darkness – individual, societal, institutional – and we must do so honestly. The much talked about openness and transparency must apply at all levels.

Irish society has tended to present itself as a light to the world. In the past this applied to our missionary zeal, emphasising the angelic nature of our humanity. Today it applies to our corporate world and economic development. We cannot suppress the darkness if we want to open to the world of the spirit. Acknowledging our vulnerability and fragility as part of the human condition is essential if we are to reconnect with the life of the Spirit.

This must be done as individuals but also as a society which has symptoms of a soullessness all around. The individual, the family, the community – are all in need of urgent attention. Injustice, inequity, family and community breakdown, drugs and crime are rampant in a society which is experiencing economic boom. The causes of these must be identified.

Our society has been working hard and successfully at the business of production. However, our passion for technological products has far outstripped the human, spiritual and social needs of our people. It has devoted vast resources to evaluating, researching and developing technological and hard products. Few resources have been made available to research, evaluate and apply that which makes us better able to relate to one another.

As we approach the new millennium we need to be working on closer integration of our economic, social and spiritual spheres. We need to be working or putting in place a society which is socially worth living in. Who gives meaning to life? Where do our values come from? These immediately raise questions about the role of the Churches. Over the last two thousand years, the great organised religions proclaimed universal and eternal truths. The Enlightenment of the eighteenth century led to a gradual and partial revision of traditional religious attitudes caused by developments in the natural sciences and the widespread acceptance of critical thinking. Its effect has been to erode the influence of some traditional religions. We are now witnessing the vacuum which this has brought about.

In Ireland we are only now beginning to experience this vacuum – economic boom and spiritual hunger. The clericalised Church held sway in an Ireland that was truly pastoral and agricultural to the middle of this century. But all this has changed.

The clericalisation of the Irish Church led to a form of religion in which there has been high compliance but little engagement; high levels of practice but low levels of reflection and the confusion of habitual ritual with deep spirituality. As we move towards the new millennium, by a strange paradox the decline in vocations to the priesthood and religious life could be the catalyst which allows the Church to play its prophetic role in restoring the religious experience to the people.

Influence of the global economy and media

There is now a two-way pulling of our national roots: in one way by globalisation and in the other by the demands of local communities and individuals for greater participation and freedom. There is no denying which is in the ascendant, so the challenge is to restore the balance by rediscovering the local as a rich resource in its own right and to rediscover relationships with self, one another, creation and the Creator.

Globalisation, in its recent form dates back to 1944 when the leading industrial nations – economists, bankers, corporate leaders – came together to institute a form of economic activity and control they said would be beneficial. The benefits initially spread to many countries and fifty years on they have reached Ireland.

However, great expectation has led to despair for many and after fifty years the experiment is breaking down. Rather than leading to economic benefits for all, it has brought the planet to the brink of environmental and social catastrophe. With the crisis now obvious in Asia, Russia, Brazil, Mexico and soon, predictably in other nations, including western industrial nations, many peoples and nation-states have begun to recognise the failure of globalisation.

Though the current crisis tends to be reported as strictly 'financial' in nature, the problems, of course, are deeper. All peoples of the world have been made dependent upon the arbitrary, self-interested acts of giant corporations, bankers and speculators. Real economic power is removed from nations, communities and people's organisations, while giving new powers to corporate and financial speculators.

The global system depends for its success on a never-ending expansion of markets, resources and consumers. This cannot survive very long. There is only so much we can consume and when this is confined to those who can pay the result is serious social inequity.

Ireland is now very vulnerable. There is no need to spell out just how linked Ireland is to the world economy. At one level, in ten short years we've come from a 'no jobs, loads of flats' to a 'plenty of jobs, where to live?' paradox. Nothing could better symbolise a booming economy than this mutation.

On the other hand, by giving up the power to direct exchange and interest rate policy we will become as umbilically tied to the EU as we are to the big corporations for jobs. We are now very vulnerable. Fruit of the Loom in Donegal and Krups in Limerick cited global conditions as the reason for shedding large numbers of jobs or closing, while a fall in demand in Russia is largely behind the farmer's immediate plight.

There is an obvious need now to balance globalisation with a move towards localisation, re-empower communities, place human, social, personal and ecological values above economic values (and corporate profit), encourage self and community reliance (wherever possible), move more and more towards the development of indigenous resources and operate in a fully democratic and transparent manner.

And are we beginning to witness the beginning of the end of Irish media? Such has been the rate of change in technology in the last two decades that it is difficult to envisage the extent of the change in the next two. By the year 2020, one can imagine where the technological revolution will leave us. With the growth of satellite and digital television we may be able to receive anything up to two hundred channels. What has the Murdoch world in store for us? Who will control television and the newspapers? And what are the values implicit in the power of popular culture?

The rediscovery of the local community and spirituality

There could be a very special role for Ireland in the Europe of the new millennium in that we have come from a spiritual and mystical past, closely connected to Creation and Creator and, for now, at least, have become strong economically. How we rediscover our sense of soul/roots/place/people could now be our great challenge. More and more people believe we need to combine economic success with spirituality and justice.

In opening the Conference President Mary McAleese reminded us 'This is a time for vision and a time for hope... . Against the background of constant change in Ireland individuals and groups throughout the country are working for the development of their communities.'

Mary Redmond, delivering the final lecture said: 'It is social entrepreneurs (voluntarism) who will provide the "alternative vision" that is needed to complement the information society. In the Community and voluntary sector soul is alive and feeling. By "soul" I mean moral or emotional or intellectual life, spirituality.' Ireland and Europe must search for a soul. In the face of globalisation we might feel powerless but we can influence the direction in which we go. We are floating on world currents but we must find ways of contributing and we must work to form partnerships and to get the balance right. There has to be a firm commitment to the local dimension. To further their thinking there was a powerful call from Professor Joe Lee for Institutes of Technology to 'go in the direction of thinking of themselves as major reflectors of nature, of their communities,' as well as equipping people for employment. Teachers are crucial in preparing people and challenging and being challenged as to where ideas are coming from. Joe Lee would argue 'that one of the main weaknesses in our public discourses is that we have too little sustained debate about philosophies of the good society in our media.' We need to stand back from the tide and constantly ask 'What are the values behind what we are doing and how do we spread those values, infiltrate them, and make them at least part of the debate?'

A sense of place is a sense of relating to others. It is a psychological as well as a physical concept. It is about a cluster of connections and relationships. It is about connecting to a people and it is vital we start linking the generations together. If we do not link the young, the middle-aged and the old then we have no society and we have no place. 'A sense of place means a sense of society for everybody', Joe Lee concluded.

The changes we – one generation – are now experiencing in Ireland and called on to cope with, took place over three to four generations in other western societies. The changes taking place in families, in communities and in individuals in our society are extraordinary. To some extent we are coping well in that we still have 'cushions' in the form of voluntarism, and a deep spiritual heritage. We have the mountains, the valleys, the hills, the lakes and the sea. We have the villages and the towns and a people who care for one another. To build on these strengths, to develop a sense of belonging could be our challenge for the future.

Conclusion

The Conference identified a theme upon which many people are focusing in the privacy of their own lives – what are we about? where exactly is the rapid pace of change leading us? Are we forgetting something? Words such as community, spiritual experience, partnership, balance and integration kept cropping up throughout the three days.

In a sense the Conference was about widening the debate, about posing questions, rather than coming up with answers and in this, it would appear it was extremely successful. Marie

Martin, from Omagh, Chairperson for the first day, probably summed up the general feeling. 'Viewed from the chair, the Conference was "like no other" in many ways. That first day brought together some of the finest speakers it has ever been my privilege to hear, and raised very high expectations – which were subsequently fulfilled – for the second and third day.'

For me the most powerful message from the Conference was how we all need to be attentive to the reality of what is going on in people's lives and in the wider society.

Following each address we allowed some time for reflection, on what had been presented and we asked the delegates to write down any question or thought which came to them at that time. We are including some of the responses which we received over the course of the three days, in this publication.

Thanks

There are very many people whose combined efforts helped to make our Conference such a success. I'm most grateful to President Mary McAleese who willingly agreed to perform the official opening and whose inspiring opening address set the tone for the Conference. We were privileged to have a most distinguished panel of speakers, each of whom, made such telling contributions – Sr Thérèse, Abbess of the Poor Clare Monastery, Ennis, John Lonergan, Governor, Mountjoy Prison, Mark Patrick Hederman, Glenstal Abbey, Professor Joe Lee, University College Cork, Tom Mc Gurk, well-known journalist and broadcaster, David McWilliams, senior economist and strategist, Professor John Drew, Durham University, David Begg, CEO, Concern Worldwide, and Mary Redmond, solicitor and founder of the Irish Hospice Foundation.

Our chairpersons: Marie Martin, Omagh, John Quinn, RTÉ, and Michael Kenny, St Patrick's College, Maynooth, were remarkable, and apart from their excellent control of proceedings also contributed in no small way to the debate.

On the organisational side a very dedicated conference committee, most of whom were involved in a voluntary capacity, put many hours, over many months, into planning and preparation and augmented by a small army of other volunteers for the duration of the Conference, ensured that everything went like clockwork. A special word of gratitude is extended to the sisters at the Poor Clare Monastery, Ennis for their prayers and support.

We are also grateful for the considerable media coverage of the event as well as for the promotional and publicity work done on behalf of the Conference by James Morrissey of Fleischman Hillard Saunders.

To everyone who attended as delegates and who brought so much to the proceedings, we say thanks. To the management and staff of the West County Hotel, Ennis, the Conference venue, we also extend our gratitude as we do to all who provided sponsorship or other forms of support.

We have had many requests to know if there will be another Conference this year, and I am happy to report that plans are already in train for Conference '99.

OPENING ADDRESS

President Mary McAleese

I am delighted to be in Ennis with you this evening and to have the honour of opening this important Conference, coming as it does as we approach the end of a century which has seen tremendous changes in society, and on the threshold of a millennium that sees us starting from a very strong economic and political base. Indeed, all of the economic analysts and the commentators tell us that we have never had it so good. Wealth creation, employment, the output of goods and services, access to credit and the acquisition of material possessions are all growing steadily – and all the indicators are that we can look forward to further prosperity.

In tandem with that prosperity, the pace and pressure of modern life are accelerating and bringing fundamental changes to society. These changes impact on every individual, family and community. While policy-makers confront the pressing challenges of the day, fundamental questions need to be asked about the long-term trends in society – and how they impact on our traditions, values and quality of life.

Given our economic and cultural achievements in recent years we are very well placed to plan for the future and to influence the shape of society and the lifestyle that the next generation will enjoy. While all of us are aware of the relentless efforts made by Government with the social partners to tackle the problems of disadvantage through a variety of special measures and programmes – the problems of exclusion and marginalisation still remain for some and, paradoxically, can be made more acute because of the high rate of development. It is important, therefore, that we maintain the focus on meeting the requirements of the most needy in our society, who can feel that they are on the outside, without a voice or a real input to the decision-making process that affects their everyday lives.

This conference provides a useful forum to address these and the many other issues that we face. This is a time for vision and a time for hope. We see how much has been achieved in Northern Ireland in recent months that has given real hope of a lasting peace on our island – where reconciliation and community work created the climate for political leaders to take bold steps – to make compromises and to hold their nerve in the run-up to the Good Friday Agreement. For the first time we have reached a comprehensive agreement between all the people of Ireland and Britain about our political future, embracing our identities and aspirations. It has transformed the situation and led to a new mood of optimism.

The referendum of 22 May was the first occasion since 1918 when the people in Ireland voted together to decide their political future – and the massive endorsement has given the Agreement and the people the strength to move forward with conviction and determination. It does not threaten traditions, identity or political aspirations, In reaching this comprehensive political agreement, all sides can be winners. In all this work of formulating, implementing and building on the Agreement, the continued support and encouragement from overseas has been vital. We know that out friends across the world have willed us to succeed.

Against the background of constant change in Ireland, individuals and groups throughout the country are working for the development of their communities. Many of you will be familiar with the work of John Canon Hayes, who founded Muintir na Tíre over sixty years ago with the aim of eliminating conflict and sectional interests in favour of a unified community-based approach to resolving problems.

We have a long and proud tradition of community activity in Ireland. We take great pride in our origins and our sense of loyalty to the people and the place from which we come. It is not at all surprising that this should express itself in concern for the common good in the form of voluntary and community service. Given the rapidly changing social and economic situation, particularly in rural areas, this commitment is even more relevant and valuable today.

It is appropriate that we should be here in Ennis – the 'Information Age' town – for the Conference. Ennis is also home to a music and heritage centre which cultivates the rich musical tradition of the country – so it faces a unique opportunity and challenge in combining its role as a leader in the information age and as a guardian of our heritage and culture – something indeed which is a challenge for all of us.

We often think of society as a block of people all sharing the same ideas and beliefs. In reality, of course, the truth is very different. Society is an association of individuals with varying ideas, beliefs and views who live and work together in co-operation for the common good. While culture or historical experience may create a common identity it should not be at the expense of minority groups or the individual. The recognition of group and individual identities is essential to underpinning a society based on equality and social justice within the community.

That spirit of community has been fostered and developed over the last twenty-five years or more by Fr Harry Bohan – through his involvement in, for example, the Rural Housing Organisation – and more recently in the LEADER Programme here in Clare – reflecting his belief in community development based on a deep appreciation of local heritage and tradition. I want to congratulate Fr. Harry Bohan and everyone associated with organising this Conference and I wish you well in your deliberations.

REFLECTION

Then said a rich man, Speak to us of Giving.
And he answered:
  You give but little when you give of your possessions.
        It is when you give of yourself that you truly give.
            For what are your possessions but things you
keep and guard for fear you may need them tomorrow?
            And tomorrow, what shall tomorrow bring to
the over-prudent dog burying bones in the trackless
sand as he follows the pilgrims to the holy city?
                And what is fear of need but need itself?
        Is not dread of thirst when your well is full, the
thirst that is unquenchable?
            There are those who give little of the much
which they have – and they give it for recognition
and their hidden desire makes their gifts unwholesome.
        And there are those who have little and give it all.
            These are the believers in life and the bounty
of life, and their coffer is never empty.

Kahlil Gibran

PART 1
A SOUL FOR IRELAND –
A SOUL FOR EUROPE

1

A SOUL FOR SOCIETY

Sr Thérèse

Introduction

In case there are any questions arising in your minds as to why I am here, I assure you it is with even greater urgency I ask myself, 'Why Am I Here?'. I am a Poor Clare contemplative nun. By free and deliberate choice I live an 'enclosed' life, totally dedicated to prayer and contemplation. One does not leave this enclosure except in exceptional circumstances, for example medical reasons, death of a parent – or a conference such as this. This is an exceptional circumstance and I am here because I believe passionately in the contemplative life and its powerful and irreplaceable contribution to society, especially as we approach the third millennium. I am here too, because Fr Harry Bohan asked me to come. I wish I could say it was his magnetic personality that drew me. No, rather it was his deep care, for our land, our people, our culture – his well-grounded fears that we are in danger of losing something very precious and his conviction that something can be done about it. No longer can we sit on the fence and lament the direction life is taking – lament the family breakdown – lament the suicides of our young and their drug abuse – lament the Omagh Bombing and other such atrocities. Such lamentations bring no relief! Hopefully we are all here because we care and care enough and maybe this conference is really about life and its meaning and about the sowing of seeds – seeds of hope for a better world.

The Irish scene

In the recent past we lived in a world of institutions or structures, in Church and in State. Now we live in a world of corporations and financial institutions backed by the media. Do we regard ourselves as belonging to an economy or to a country? Are we part of the machinery of a government or are we a people, a culture? In religious terms, do we belong to an institutional Church or to a believing community of caring and sharing? Who or what shapes our thinking, our attitudes? Is it the corporate world, the media or a materialistic society which refuses to question anything – its focus is on money and the more of it? These are the questions we need to ask ourselves, lest we lose the greatest treasure we as a people have – our spiritual heritage.

Who is leading us?

On the international scene it is good to be Irish right now. Our athletes, our musicians, our scholars have excelled themselves and we feel a legitimate pride and joy in their achievements. On the home front, we are experiencing an incredible economic growth and that is so good. But what if this economic growth, this boom leads to bust, what then will sustain us? We hear so much about the Celtic Tiger, but the tiger is a rare species and dangerous when provoked. Could it be that we are slowly being led, directed or controlled by this tiger, which by the way is anything but celtic! Our celtic ancestors appreciated the presence and compassion of an all-powerful, ever-close God. They loved the land, they loved nature and had an awesome sense of community values. Celtic Tiger? This is an unhappy liaison.

Despite all the signs of progress and prosperity, disillusionment is a harsh reality for many. Why has prosperity not brought the peace and security we long for so much? It would seem society itself is out of touch with its own soul or, in the warning of Vaclav Havel, 'The modern person has lost his or her transcendental anchor and along with it the only genuine source of responsibility and self respect.' Maybe it's time for us to listen again to the prophet Jeremiah:

Halt at the crossroads, look well and see which path led you in good stead long ago. That path follow and you will have life.

The contemplative's message

What then has the contemplative to say to this disillusioned society? Condemn me if you will for my simplicity but it is my firm belief that society is dispirited and disillusioned because by and large we are living, 'outside of ourselves'. Cut off from our true selves, from our own deepest centre, we find ourselves cut off from God, our neighbour and nature itself – disconnected, alienated – and deep loneliness is the result. How well we camouflage this alienation, this loneliness, as we climb the ladder of so-called success. The witness and the call of the contemplative life is to 'come back' – to come back to one's own heart, one's own deepest centre and 'live' from within there. Don't switch off from me now! This is not just about me, the contemplative, this is about *you* – the contemplative dimension in you. It is my invitation and my challenge to you all here today, to move into your own hearts, your own deepest centre and live out of there. If you do then everything will look different, and I mean *everything*! When we don't we are living on the surface, in the control of forces outside of ourselves, and that is not living, that is slavery. Carl Jung puts it well when he says:

> Your vision will become clear only when you can look into your heart. Who looks outside, dreams, who looks inside, awakes.

Having said then that society seems to be living outside of itself, controlled even, by forces outside of itself – and that the living witness and the call of the contemplative is a call to come back to one's heart, to live from within – I need to emphasise that this is not just my own idea. If we are sick, we go to a doctor or a specialist, if we have a legal problem we go to a lawyer – we go to the expert in that particular field. When it comes to the subject of life, where can one go except to the source – God, the one who gave us life – and to his Son, Jesus, who came to show us how to live that life and live it to the full.

I will illustrate for you what I mean by 'living from within' through a simple Gospel story – the story about Jesus meeting a Samaritan woman at Jacob's Well.

This story has profound messages about 'living water' – about Jesus revealing himself as the Messiah and about Jesus inviting this woman to look into her heart. There in her heart she finds the courage to be so truthful – 'I have no husband,' she tells Jesus – in fact she had five!

This 'going into our hearts' is what I want to speak to you about. And now for the story!

Jesus and his disciples are making a journey from Judea to Galilee and in order to do so they have to pass through the hostile territory of Samara. It is hot and he is very tired. His disciples, big burly fishermen that they were, well seasoned by sun and storm see this, go on ahead into the town for food, leaving him to rest by the well – Jacob's Well.

A woman comes along, a Samaritan woman. She is not called poor, but in every sense of the word she is a poor woman, for she has had five husbands. To be rejected or forsaken even once, they say, is an incredibly painful experience. How then does this woman feel who has been used, abused and rejected five times, and is this just a round figure? How would any one of us feel? She is raw, she is wounded, she is fragile in her deepest centre, her heart – so what does she do? She erects a barrier around her pain and chooses to live 'outside of herself' on the surface – there on the surface at least she can be free of pain – it's her only safe place. But living on the surface leaves her wide open to her so-called lovers – her users. She is in their control.

Jesus engages her in conversation – how well she handles this conversation, from her 'safe place'. He asks for water and how quickly the reply comes back. He speaks then about 'living water', and her response here is swift as well, whatever living water might mean for her! He then asks her to fetch her husband and there had to be a stab of pain here, and embarrassment too – but she keeps face and then veers off in another direction. We find her talking about worshipping God on this mountain or on that, and then on to the Messiah and who he might be. We have to marvel at how this poor woman is drawing such revelations from Jesus. We have to marvel too, at the way he empowers her to stay with him in the conversation. All the time he is leading the conversation deeper and deeper but she is keeping ever more firmly entrenched on the surface. As I said, she handles this conversation well and who could guess what was happening inside her – but something did because when the disciples return with the food, she slips away quietly and runs back to the town to tell everyone about her meeting.

And what did she tell them? About the living water? About his identity as Messiah? No! But referring to the short sentence in the middle of this profound conversation she says, 'Come and see someone who has told me everything I ever did'. Now, remember, these townspeople would have shunned this woman. She was after all a loose woman but now there is no shame or grovelling on her part. And why? Because for the first time in her life, someone has seen her as she really is and still loved her. Don't we all know this ache, to be seen as we really are and still be loved? She is wounded, she is raw, fragile and sinful, but she has not been judged or condemned. Far from it. Love and compassion flow from the heart of Jesus, leading her back, through her barrier, right back into her own heart, into her own deepest centre where she can and must be healed. And healed she was, and freed too. Her dignity now restored, she can face those who have shunned her. She doesn't hug the experience to herself – she wants them to be gifted as she has been gifted and this caring and sharing comes from the heart of one who is in touch with oneself and with the God who dwells within. Yes, Jesus led her back into her own heart/soul as to an oasis. Henceforth, her deepest centre would be a place of peace and refreshment and her yearning would be that others would experience this same gift. God, oneself, one's neighbour – she was integrated and reconnected – she belonged again.

Isn't this what we all need? To get back in touch with our hearts, with our own soul – to begin to make the right connections in and with our lives. It is then, surely, that we would see ourselves as persons in search of community rather than cogs in the mis-named Celtic Tiger wheel.

And within each one of us there should be such an oasis, a place of refreshment and peace and this brings me to the whole subject of contemplation. What is it? In a nutshell, it's about those things we all long for so much, search for too – but in the wrong place. It's about a deep and abiding joy and peace that comes from the experience of being loved by God, and I stress that word 'experience'. It's not an intellectual knowing but an experience similar to two people who are in love. A single glance across a room can communicate that love, without any sound or words. Or it's the difference between tasting a lovely glass of red wine and merely knowing all about it. Isn't it incredible that we can experience in this way?

Some people are called specifically to devote their entire lives to contemplation. These respond in a very real way to Christ's invitation to, 'Come away by yourselves to a lonely place'. It is not, however, a call to loneliness. Rather, it is a call to closeness, closeness to God, to oneself, to one's neighbour, to nature and to how well Irish spirituality of old understood that reality – how well preceding generations lived it. They were truly contemplative. One only has to recall the greeting of the passerby to the workers, 'God bless the work', or on entering a house, 'God bless all here'. Blessings flow from the heart of one who is in touch with one's self and with one's God and where could they flow except to the neighbour.

It was Dag Hammarskjöld who once said 'the longest journey on earth is the journey inwards'. And those who devote their lives entirely to contemplation embark on this journey in a very real way. Outwardly, the contemplative life appears as a life of utter simplicity. About six to seven hours each day are spent in prayer and outside of that time the members of a community are engaged in very simple and ordinary work so that the prayer spills over and gradually transforms the whole day into one long prayer. What cannot be observed however, is the inner life, the inner journey that goes on within the heart of each one. Leaving the world and entering a monastery is only the first step – leaving the 'world within' is the real challenge. We all have a world of hopes, dreams, desires, ambitions and jealousies within us and if I suggested that we stop right here and observe a few moments of silence just to get in touch with our inner selves, I wonder what would we find? Would there be more turmoil within than all the noise outside of us?

On the inward journey, all this has to be confronted, named and relinquished because this call to become totally poor within is so that one can create an inner space for God – so that one can gain, as it were, power over his heart – and maybe that is why monasteries are often called 'powerhouses of prayer'. Those relatively few people who embark on this way of life do not do so for themselves – their agonies, their ecstasies are for others. Their inner freedom and their deep love equip them to stand before God on behalf of the whole world – to stand before him in praise, thanksgiving and intercession. This intercession is a feeling of a solidarity with the pain, the anxiety and the hopelessness that many in our society experience. We contemplatives see ourselves 'at one' with all society's pain and joy and our dwelling-place is an oasis of peace and refreshment.

Contemplatives in the world

What then of the rest of us? The truth is, we all have a spiritual or contemplative dimension to our lives and it is precisely because this is so undernourished that everything else falls out of place, resulting in confusion and disillusionment, if not outright chaos.

We are so aware of our physical life and all our glossy magazines tell us in so many ways how to care for and pamper the body. But we also have an emotional life and, judging from the increase in marital and family breakdown, it is in a state of chaos. We have an intellectual life as well, but holding them all together at their centre is the life of the Spirit – our 'contemplative dimension' – and this should be an oasis of peace and refreshment because whether we believe it or not, God is there.

Most of us at some time in our lives have stood before an open coffin and contemplated the 'remains' of someone we have known – and how apt the expression the 'remains'. As we look on, we know for certain that the real person is not there – the bodily remains are, but the spirit, the soul, has gone out or gone on, into eternity. How then do we spend so much time feeding and pampering the body which eventually goes down into the earth and so little time on the spirit which will live for ever and ever?

Our world is God's gift to us. Our country, our land with its people and its culture is his gift to each one of us. The salvation of this human world lies nowhere else than in the human heart and in its power to reflect with meekness and responsibility – out of the integrity of its own soul. We need to care for life, to nurture it, to develop it, to beautify it, but how can we do this if we don't pause to see which way we are going, pause to think of the giver of the gift and what his intentions might be? And when we do pause, what do we see? We see that we are living in a world of rapid change.

We are told the generation gap is down now to five years instead of fifty – the pace of life is swift!

We are living in a competitive society where the person who hesitates is definitely lost – the pace of life is risky!

We are living in a materialistic society where all that matters is that the goods are delivered no matter what the cost – the pace of life can be cruel!

Practical suggestions

How can I get off the treadmill? How can I get in touch with my deepest centre – my spirit? There is no easy way. Choices have to be made. Do I choose my work, my promotion, my salary increase, the bigger car... to the detriment of my own inner peace, my spouse, my family and quality time spent with them? Can I take time to admire a sunset and say 'Thank you, God,' or just be with a lonely or elderly person and let them know I care. As I said, choices have to be made. Am I living from within and in control of my life, or am I on the surface, 'outside of myself', like the Samaritan woman, and therefore in the control of the system, the corporation, whatever!

One thing is certain – our lives can never have any depth, quality, peace, or any measure of real success, unless we set aside at least fifteen to twenty minutes a day to be with ourselves and to get in touch with what is going on in our deepest centre – our spirit – to get in touch with God. As great as our need is to get in touch with our inner self, 'our contemplative dimension', is our need to have quality in-depth conversation to nourish and encourage us on our journey. We could say too that what we feed our minds on is what we pray about. What are we feeding our minds on – what is the quality of our reading and how does it influence our lives, our prayer?

Simple suggestions, but incredibly difficult to put into practice. They require great discipline. It is hard to be still, it is hard to go against the tide but it is our sure road back to peace and serenity and our sure way of restoring the balance in society

Seeds of hope

Achievement, prosperity and deep disillusionment have been

spoken about. What I haven't mentioned is the almost phenomenal spiritual hunger that is emerging almost as a result. Our community would be very aware of this from the people who come to us – why else would one go to a monastery unless in search of spiritual food? Last year at a time when we as a community were discerning our community vision for the year 2000, Fr Harry and his staff from RRD approached us. Appreciating our contemplative stance and with deep reverence for our way of life, they asked if we had anything to share with them that might deepen and enrich their lives – insisting however, that it would not harm our chosen vocation in any way. They needed us to be truly contemplative.

It seems providential in a sense, that they came to us at a time when we were discerning our own way forward as a centre of spirituality, which John Paul II has encouraged our houses to be. We were naming our need to be more contemplative than ever for the sake of our world, and yet asking ourselves had we anything to share with the spiritually hungry, without taking away from our contemplative stance. As a result, our two groups meet on a monthly basis. We discuss life's priorities. We have private reflection. The Bible, of course, is the daily bread of all contemplatives, but now both groups have begun to use the Bible for inspiration and enlightenment, all of which is gathered in a community conversation giving us direction for the following month. This is a mutual Poor Clare/ RRD enrichment as we, for our part, appreciate the need and the urgency for the contemplative dimension in the marketplace – and our RRD friends hopefully receive some insight from our contemplative way of life. This is a 'seed of hope' and hopefully many other seeds of hope will be sown as a result of this conference.

The spiritual hunger I spoke of assures us that our inner journey has already begun. We as a people don't have to go out in search of our soul – we have to come back home and drink from the same well within us as our ancestors did of old. They were so conscious of the soul as the divine spark within themselves. This divine spark sang out from their hearts:

> Christ with me – Christ within me
> Christ behind me – Christ before me
> Christ in quiet – Christ in danger
> Christ in hearts of all that love me
> Christ in mouth of friend and stranger.

And isn't this in the same vein as what Vaclav Havel says we need to explore? 'To see the very earth we inhabit linked with heaven above us'. In conclusion, I leave you with this nugget of monastic wisdom:

> Once upon a time, an ancient monastic tale says, the Elder said to the business person, 'As the fish perishes on dry land, so you perish when you get entangled in the world. The fish must return to the water and you must return to the Spirit.' And the business person was aghast. 'Are you saying that I must give up my business and go into a monastery?' he asked. And the Elder said, 'Definitely not. I am telling you to hold on to your business and go into your heart'.

2

CLIMBING INTO OUR PROPER DARK – IRELAND'S PLACE IN EUROPE

Mark Patrick Hederman OSB

The theme of this conference is 'Our Society in the New Millennium – Are we Forgetting Something?' My contribution concerns 'the dark'. The first half of my title, 'Climbing Into Our Proper Dark' is taken from a line in one of Seamus Heaney's poems and needs some introduction.

When we talk about the dark, the underground, the unconscious, we are using metaphors. The dark, the shadow, the night-time realm of the unconscious, represents the part of ourselves we can never reach in broad daylight, as a tourist or a traveller with a guide book and map. Metaphor is the way we talk about what we don't know, what is invisible, unavailable to us, using words that describe what is ordinary or familiar. Metaphor is the language of poetry, which we can use when we come to the edge of normal discourse. When our fingers can no longer touch the walls of the place we are trying to enter, metaphors act, almost like extensions of our fingernails, as bridges to the rockface beyond our reach. That is why poetry has always been one door into the dark.

When I use the word 'dark' here it is as an image. The image is, of course, based on a reality which we all know, which is then used to point out another reality, which we do not know as well. But let me remind you of the reality we do know. We don't need much reminding in this country. This last week has been a guided tour. Every day darker than the next. The Romans, when they got here from sunny Italy, thought it was winter all the time, so they called it Hibernia, from their word for winter, *hibernus*. Last Christmas most of us were, literally, in the dark. It gave us something to talk about, during the endless parties of the Christmas Season. 'How did you manage? How did you cook the turkey? What did you do for light?' We were in total darkness for the whole of the festivities. It reminded us how dependent we are on electrification for so much of what we do.

'Rural electrification'. The catch-cry of the 1950s. You'd remember the dark if you had to do all those jobs before electric light came in: trimming the wick, cleaning the globe (if you'll excuse the pun), filling the lamps with oil. Listen to William Mangan in *An Irish Boyhood in Westmeath* in 1918:

> In the winter, going to bed meant going by candlelight. It was something you did not do alone. We knew all about ghosts and spooks and witches, and giants too. And a shakily held flickering candle on dark stairs or in the board-creaking blackness of a terrifying tunnel or passage, could cast moving spectral shadows, that would turn your flesh cold and stand hair on the back of your neck on end. So, to give ourselves courage, we went up the stairs in a body, clutching the grown-ups' hands.

Bansha was one of the first places to get electrified in 1947, fifty years ago. It was a pilot scheme and it was voluntary. You didn't have to get it, if you thought it was a bad idea. Wiring was charged to the people, but the parish paid for those on the dole and those living in cottages. It came to the shops in town first. One man came back from the shop where it had just been installed, full of wonder.

> 'There's a bottle hanging down from the ceiling,' he said, 'and the light is in that, and it floods the whole place in brightness'.
> 'How do you get it to work?' his wife asked him.
> 'Well, you just go over and scratch the wall up and down and the light comes on in the bottle.'

The end of the candle era – the new breakthrough into light. Now, as we approach the millennium, we are beginning to live in a world that has forgotten what darkness is. New York, 'the city that never sleeps', is ablaze twenty-four hours a day. On my first trip to Brussels in 1980, I was collected at the airport at ten o'clock at night by an octogenarian who drove his car without headlights through the city, until stopped by a policeman. The city is so well lit at night – as indeed is the whole country – we hadn't even noticed.

Well, this is the reality that, I am suggesting, we do have to notice. And I don't just mean the physical reality of the dark. I mean the psychological reality, the darkness inside each one of us. We spend much of our lives asleep. This night-time realm of our unconscious is the one we have to approach and 'climb into' .The words 'climbing into' are also 'poetic'. They describe a way of reaching the dark that requires energetic effort. There are barriers, there is a necessity to surmount these.

In the early 1960s, when we had reached the peak of our rural electrification and the pinnacle of scientific conquest of the universe, most of us sat up for the whole of one night watching the first man to put his foot on the moon. There were two of them, in fact. 'One small step for man, one giant step for mankind,' we remember it well. Some people didn't have television at the time, so they gathered in the houses that did. A group were sitting spell-bound in this farmer's kitchen listening to Kevin O'Kelly and watching Neil Armstrong's foot. The farmer's wife was fussing around the kitchen cleaning and fetching.

> 'Will you for God's sake sit down, woman and watch what's happening. You will never again see the likes of this as long as you or I live'.
> She replied, 'Ah sure, who'd be bothered with that. They're always somewhere, climbing and rooting.'

There are a number of ways to 'climb into' the dark of our unconscious. The first way is by being attentive to our dreams. We dream every night but we may not be aware of it. It takes time and attention to let ourselves become aware of these dreams. They are the language of our unconscious telling us what we refuse to tell ourselves during our daylight hours. Nor are they easy to interpret. We have to learn to crack the code. Most of us are both afraid and dismissive of the dark side of ourselves. We anaesthetise ourselves with sleeping pills or alcohol. Whether we kill the dark with drugs or drink or work or entertainment or sleep, the method achieves the same result – it cuts us off from an essential aspect of our lives and ourselves. And it is so easy to imagine that this cutting off is a good thing, that light means good and dark means bad and to draw for ourselves an evolutionary trajectory whereby we move from the 'Dark Ages' upwards and onwards to the age of enlightenment. Such momentum might even tempt us to hope that by the millennium we would have wiped out the darkness altogether. Zero tolerance towards unlit streets.

One of Ireland's tasks in Europe of the next century must be to remind ourselves and to remind all Europeans that we carry the dark around with us, that it is an essential part of our make-up, that we never shake it off and move onwards, that we don't become children of light, that there is no such thing as progress towards complete incandescence, that in a memorable phrase of Herbert Butterfield, each one of us remains 'equidistant from barbarity'. And that is the way it should be. The Mexicans called the European men 'Hombre', from the shadow they cast. The word, like the word 'umbrella', comes from the Latin for shadow. Our role in Europe is to remind us of that definition, that reality of the shadow which we also are.

Seven per cent of the world's land mass and 15 per cent of its population are descendants of Europa: the peoples of Europe. It is not numerically or physically large. Apart from Australia, it is the smallest continent. However, the influence it has had on the planet is gigantic and indelible. Europe has been largely responsible for the way the world is today and much of that history is the result of Europe's failure to understand, appropriate and deal with the shadow side of itself.

Apart from our own dream time, there is also the great reminder of this reality contained in the stories of our ancestors. What dreams are to individuals, myths and legends are to peoples. The Irish have one of the greatest storehouses of such commentaries on our Celtic unconscious, a mythology that is the admiration and the envy of other tribes. But such a storehouse exists for all of us as Europeans and it is from this particular source that 1 want to draw.

> I met a man here last night who saw my badge and said, 'Are you giving a talk here tomorrow?'
> I said 'Yes.'
> 'Well,' he said, 'I won't be here. I'm going to a bull market in Kilmallock.'
> 'Well,' I said, 'If you only knew – that's exactly where I'm trying to bring these people tomorrow morning!'

And so I begin with the famous legend of Theseus who came to Crete and, with the help of Ariadne, daughter of the king, slew the Minotaur, half-man, half-bull, who consumed boatloads of young people every year. Europa (after whom our continent was named) was the grandmother of this Minotaur. Ireland's role in Europe during the next century, to put it in a nutshell, could be to act as another Ariadne to Europe's grandchildren.

So let us examine the myth of Europe more closely. Zeus/Jupiter, father of the Gods, married Europa. He came to her disguised as a white bull 'not with fiery eyes and lowered horns' one account tells us, 'but gently, as if to express a mute request'. The white bull carried her off to the land which he named 'Europe' after her and there they gave birth to a son, Minos.

Minos, the son of Europa, married Pasiphae who later developed 'a monstrous passion' – for a bull. The offspring of that passion was the Minotaur, 'a monster half-human, half-bull' who fed exclusively on human flesh. A prison-palace was constructed for him from which no one could find an exit. They called it the Labyrinth. Here the monster fed on supplies of youths owed to Minos as tribute from neighbouring, non-EU members.

Eventually that great slayer of monsters, Theseus, arrives and turns his attentions to the Minotaur, 'the monster of the dark.' He is helped by the daughter of Minos, Ariadne, who, it is sometimes forgotten, is Pasiphae's unmonstrous offspring and sister to the Minotaur. She falls in love with Theseus and before he enters the Labyrinth gives him a sword and a ball of silken thread which he ties to the entrance and which then leads him out again after he has slain the Minotaur.

In this blessed twentieth century we have begun to crack the code of these dreamlike sequences, we have revisited the labyrinth and have begun to rehabilitate the Minotaur. We have understood that gods and goddesses placed by antiquity in the heavens above or in the depths of the ocean below are to be discovered inside ourselves, deep in our own intestinal labyrinths. And the bull is ourselves at our most vital, our most dangerous, our most horny. And the minotaur is the way we have described the monstrous conjunction of these aspects of ourselves with the human, the angelic, the divine. We have reviled ourselves as Minotaurs. We have created this scapegoat for the dark side of ourselves and constructed an underground labyrinth where we hide one of the most important sides of ourselves.

European culture, and particularly Irish culture since the foundation of this State as an independent entity, has been constructed over this labyrinth which has been closed off and sealed with impregnable hubcaps, leaving the reality below to fester unattended as in a pressure cooker. These ideals, on which we Europeans base the conduct of our lives, are hybrid and ancient, coming as they do from European philosophy at its deepest and most idiosyncratic. They are also very noble. They have inspired the philosophy of Plato, the intellectual mysticism of Plotinus, the Gothic cathedrals of Europe. But the trouble is that they are not us. We are made up of both shadow and light. We are irretrievably creatures of darkness as well as beacons of light. If this is not acknowledged, catered for, assumed and integrated into our full humanity, then we become dislocated, schizoid, two-timers. If, like Rochester in Jane Eyre, we lock up our mad wife in the attic, or in the labyrinth under the cellar, and pretend to ourselves and to everyone else that she does not exist, that she is not there, eventually she will escape, creep out at night and burn the house down.

The basis for this ideal stemmed from Greek philosophy. All our words to describe our world-view are Greek: politics, ethics, economy, philosophy etc. But these also became the vehicle for Christianity in many of its later formulations. The unwritten teaching of Jesus Christ became articulated in systems of thought which were available and apparently compatible. These are essentially Greek patterns of thought, although fed also by other sophisticated local cultures. The result was and is a very admirable and very beautiful explanation of the universe and of ourselves.

However, it is dangerous and detrimental when it makes serious errors of judgement about who we are, about what is essential to our natures and what is not, and, above all, what an all-powerful and all-perfect God would or would not find acceptable about our humanity. Our invitation to become 'children of God', which is what the Incarnation was all about, when transferred into this local culture, became an invitation to renounce being human and to set about becoming divine, to stop being animals and start being angels. The invitation is read as asking us to become the opposite of what we are, as human beings. If 'spiritual' is interpreted in this way it means renouncing or repudiating everything that is not spiritual, which means our nature, our flesh and, above all, our sexuality.

This, of course, could be a very different agenda from the one which Christ's Incarnation might have been offering. God's adoption of us as his children might have meant that our humanity was being vindicated and validated, that being fully human was being what God intended us to be, or as one of the first Christian teachers, Irenaeus, born in 130, has put it, 'The Glory of God is each one of us fully alive.' It could have meant that by becoming fully human we would thereby become holy.

The danger of so ambiguous a message is that it can be interpreted as renunciation of our humanity. In order to measure up to the sublime invitation which has been offered, the least you can do is make yourselves as bright, shiny and respectable as possible. Renunciation is the way to achieve this. Renunciation of everything that is human makes you more and more 'divine.' Such renunciation in terms of the vows of chastity, poverty and obedience, for instance, were often described as 'white martydom'. Martyrdom of blood, which was red, and meant giving up your life, was the ideal way to enter the divine realm, its pale alternative was the daily doing to death of everything fleshly or bodily in you. This kind of holiness washes us whiter than white and removes us from any darkness whatever into His wonderful light, almost envisaged as a kind of liquid weed-killer, with a powerful brand-name, perpetually swirling around and scouring our newly motivated insides. 'You were washed and you were justified, you were sanctified in the name of the Lord Jesus Christ and in the Spirit of our God. We pray that this holiness may remain in us… asking by day and by night that we be preserved… in the holiness and newness of life given by his grace.'

High-pitched harangue. An address to the troops. An appeal for the highest standards. Anything less is shamed out of court. After an invitation to the holy place, who would dream of wearing muddy boots, who would have the nerve to bring anything as unsightly as galoshes or waders? Not at all. Everyone will be scrubbed clean, wear stiff collars and starched shirts. And, more ominously, if you don't accept this invitation, if you don't want to conform to its requirements, well, you can look forward to punishment for eternity. Simple as that.

The false divisions which seem to have been grafted onto the Christian event can be described as human geometries devised to formulate the comprehensive programme which early Christians believed to be based upon self-evident axioms deriving from the incarnation. Christ himself never wrote, except once in the sand. The only geometry (meaning measurement of our world) he left us is the sign of the cross. To explain the possible distortion of this geometry, which I am suggesting might have happened through its translation into the culture of the Greeks, I shall use the language of shapes and forms in mathematics (the most natural language of our human minds) to describe three shifts of emphasis which have determined the European vector, meaning that entity which has both magnitude and direction and which determines the position of one point in space relative to another.

The first such geometry woven around the cross could be described as a rhombus – an oblique equilateral parallelogram – which describes the architecture of the 'spiritual' world. The easiest way to envisage this construction is to imagine a diamond, drawn from the top of the cross to each of the arms and from each of the arms to the base. In this perception the point of incarnation is achieved with minimum insertion into the world. There is no penetration downwards from the point at the foot of the cross. Everything below this point is Hades or hell or the labyrinth of the Minotaur. All the work of salvation is filtering those who are suctioned into the space created by the immortal diamond of the cross upwards towards eternity: the unity, beauty, goodness and truth of the one true God, source and fulfilment of all that is. This cross casts no shadow, in fact all such geometries are two-dimensional. The theological syntheses of the Middle Ages were built upon this harmonious architecture, with Plato's famous line dividing the world of matter from the world of spirit, a line that travelled across the equator on the surface of the earth, and through the midriff of the human body, as the diameter of the diamond; and the Gothic spires that dotted Europe are architectural symbols of the vector, derived from such geometry. The essential rhythm of this architecture is that everything comes from one and returns to one. Everything that is, is a singular substance. We stand alone. The originating principle of this world. This architecture, this humanity, is the paragon of self-subsisting, self-sufficient, self-reliant aloneness.

The second division can be described as a parallelogram of forces. It describes two perpendicular cubes on each side of the vertical cross, one on the left and one on the right, into which have been squeezed, as into two contradictory opposite compartments, the male and the female, the masculine and the feminine, Adam and Eve, Bonnie and Clyde, Samson and Delilah, Diarmuid and Gráinne, Hansel and Gretel, Frankie and Johnny, Tristan and Isolde, Romeo and Juliet, Franny and Zooey. We have created a whole alphabet of such contradistinction. Because, this law of mathematics informs us, if two forces acting at a point be represented in magnitude and direction by two sides of a parallelogram meeting at that point, then their resultant is represented by the diagonal drawn from that point. They become diametrically opposed. But it need not be so. Things could have been different. Was this meant to be the way forward from what we read of Jesus and Mary, Jesus and the woman at the well, Jesus and Veronica, Jesus and Mary Magdalene?

Finally, if we were to form a rectangle on the top part of the cross, joining the upper arms to the uppermost vertex and declare that everything good, true, bright, white, eternal, valuable, redeemed and saved is to be found within that space and that everything outside that is bad, false, dark, black, perishable, damned and useless, we would get some inkling of the third false division which circled around the newborn Christianity.

All geometry is a caricature and so are these descriptive shapes and forms. But they give us a picture of the vector created by the directive force of such ideals which we in Ireland, as inheritors of several different cultures and a somewhat oppressive history, have allowed ourselves to perpetrate or to have imposed upon us between, for instance, the masculine and the feminine, between the head and the heart, and between the individual and the community.

Ireland has represented itself to itself and to the world as a light to the nations, zealous missionaries of the angelic nature of humanity. Our more recent 'official' culture has been overly obsessed by light as opposed to darkness. We have tried to persuade ourselves at every level that we were people of light, the claidheamh solais, angels in fact. Self-sacrificing zealots have been our inspiration from the beginning of our journey as a light-house off the coast of Europe. Whether these were fighting for our freedom from the tyranny of political power, or freedom from the 'flesh', they all had the same characteristics. They were hard, upright, detached, intransigent and solitary men. This was the ideal. This was what you aimed for and dreamed of, even if you fell short. And presumably and hopefully most fell short. Because successful realisation of the ideal must have meant a lonely uninhabited existence rather like the one so vividly and depressingly portrayed by John McGahern in the character of the father in his novel and recent television serial *Amongst Women*.

Ireland was kept in the dark about the darkness. We were not the only population to have been consciously sheltered in this way by well-meaning authorities of one kind or another. But suppression of the darkness and unawareness of the unconscious, avoidance of all entrances to the underground, were helped by our being an island and by the cultural isolation which this made possible. In 1937 the De Valera Constitution of our 'free' state, with large input from John Charles McQuaid, Archbishop of Dublin, expressed this derived philosophy in no uncertain terms. In a radio broadcast to mark its first anniversary in 1938, De

Valera harangued the troops, 'A faith without good works is dead, so must we expect our Constitution to be, if we are content to leave it merely as an idle statement of principles, in which we profess belief, but have not the will to put into practice.'

Two years before that, in 1936, my mother came over to Ireland on the Cunard Line from America. Everybody in America knew that Edward VIII, King of England, was having an affair with Mrs Wallis Simpson. It was all over the newspapers, with photographs of the pair. In Ireland, and indeed England, when my mother arrived, nobody knew about it. It was a secret. The government had forbidden the Press to publish this news. It was considered dangerous to national security, and the Press obeyed. When my mother began to tell people at parties in Dublin, they thought she was off her head. Being a conscientious Catholic she asked a Jesuit priest whether it was libel, detraction or scandal to be spreading news that was common knowledge in America but completely unknown over here. 'I'm not quite sure which it is,' he said, 'but it's very interesting. Tell me more.'

Although the radio was first transmitted in 1926 and more fully so after 1930, when the booster in Athlone made it available throughout the countryside, it would have to be acknowledged that for many people in Ireland, the first glimpses they got of the door into the dark was through Gay Byrne's *Late Late Show* from the 1960s onwards.

Speaking of which and current arguments about RTÉ, it is interesting to note that during the East Clare election of 1917, when De Valera and McNeill stood shoulder to shoulder on the election platform here in Ennis, they stopped the proceedings at the appropriate time and asked a priest to say the Angelus in Irish. This event has been recorded by a local poet in terms that illustrate the atmosphere I am trying to evoke:

De Valera had spoken in manly appeal
To the gallant Dalcassians, and up stood McNeill.

And his pleading for Erin with eloquence fell,
Hark, sweet came the tones of the Angelus Bell.

A reverent pause as the sound reached his ear,
Then he called out aloud to a priest standing near;
'The Angelus, Father', and bowed was each head
As the message to God in the old tongue was said.

The geometry of 'angelism' which produces a schizoid culture builds itself out of the great divide between spirit and flesh, soul and body, mind and matter, heaven and earth. Such a topography has obsessed the European mind from the beginnings of European philosophy and although the paradigms have differed and the variations changed according to local and temporal fashion, the essential structures have remained in place.

The way you imagine you are determines the way you decide to behave. The way you decide to behave is your morality. When you believe that mind is the all-important element in your make-up, then you try to arrange for this one element to govern the rest. You install a monarchy and your life becomes a game of monopoly. In this regard it has been constantly stated that the head should rule the heart, that reason must govern the passions, that the soul must reign supreme over the body. Various strategies have been devised to effect this monopoly and implement this policy. In fact, all education must in some way succeed in controlling the untamed urges of each individual, otherwise we inevitably invite a situation of anarchy and violence. However, the mistake here is not just that mind or spirit or soul should have the authority and the power to enslave or even destroy but that any particular faculty or element of our make-up should be valorised and promoted to the detriment or destruction of any other. Integration of every element until harmony reigns should be what happens, as it does in an orchestra. But the easier and more efficient way is to impose the all-powerful hegemony of one dictatorial principle over all the rest. This was the fundamental choice which sprang from prevailing tendencies in the surrounding cultures and it was decisive and detrimental to the future development of European social and psychological history. It is the colonial mentality, the basis of ethnic cleansing, the *carte blanche* to kill whatever refuses to submit.

In this despotism it is not just the choice of absolute ruler that is wrong, it is the fact of despotism itself. In other words, to trace all that we are back to one or other principle is not simply wrong because it points to the wrong suspect on the identification parade, it is wrong because it seeks to reduce our multifaceted and variegated network of being to one most basic one. It is the tendency to try to trace everything back to a single Adam or a single Eve, when the reality is pluriform and multiple. The way we behave is what we call our ethics. Ethics based on this morality fails to comprehend what we are as human beings. It must surely be clear to us by now that the morality which was proposed to us, and which was meant to have been enshrined in our Constitution, simply does not fit our bill. It neither asks nor answers the right questions. When it allows some of the questions to be asked, then it might begin to move towards satisfactory and comprehensive answers, that people could recognise as viable and life-promoting. Such a morality must cease to be an 'asceticism of punitive discipline' and become what Charles Davis has called 'the asceticism of achieved spontaneity'. When we know the kind of people we were meant to be, we can summon up the courage and exercise the discipline necessary to achieve that goal. As Kierkegaard says, 'When I get to the next world I won't be asked why I was not more like Christ or anyone else, I will be asked why I was not more like myself.' No one minds renunciation that promotes life, that cuts off whatever is holding us back, renunciation as pruning. It is renunciation as punishment or as the doing to death of some part of myself that I do not want to let die which is unacceptable. Renunciation of food, of pleasure, of even life itself, all these are possible, but as Martin Buber says, 'Renunciation of being what I am is a sublime absurdity.'

No morality that forbids us even to enter the attic and examine our proper darkness can be taken seriously in present circumstances. This century has been the victim of too many people who were afraid to spring-clean this attic, refused to face the darkness, or dogmatically declared that there was no such reality as the unconscious. Their own darkness came out in spite of them and our century is scarred by the havoc then wrought. But that is historical evidence on a grand scale. Every individual life is also tainted by the leakages from an unexamined and inadequately housed shadow side.

Art provides a door into the dark. This door is a lintel, a frame, a threshold, a surface with hinges that opens into something else. Art frames a picture. The picture can be a symbol of something sensed, experienced and expressed. It can be the hidden life of the artist, life as it flows through the minutes of a day and the porous sensitivity of the one who tries to 'grasp the living passion as it rises'. The work of art is a relic of ungraspable, fleeting, but deeply registered experience. Science deals with the facts that apply to all of us, the inexorable laws governing each one of us as samples of the species. We all get wet if we plunge into water, we all break bones if we dive into cement, we all burn if we sit on a stove. Art presents us with the possibilities open to us as unique individuals. Scientific analysis of a seed reveals everything except the possibility of a flower. Art suggests to us the shape and fragrance of the flowers that can grow. It also makes us aware of what is peculiarly ourselves. Novels, poems, plays tell us articulately the things we were trying to say confusedly to ourselves, or they make us aware of what we had been oblivious to even though it had been going on in the background of our lives. Not that the experience is ever precisely the same, but it has enough echoes of our own to make us aware that something similar happened to us, and it makes us retrospectively sensitive to the texture and the repercussions.

The artist is like a spy or an explorer entering enemy territory or undiscovered lands. They leave coded signs, touchstones, sculpted shapes that describe both the direction and the contours of the journey. These 'objective correlatives' to use T.S. Eliot's phrase, their 'nerves in patterns on a screen', help us to find, monitor and express for ourselves, our own charting of the way through life. One of the subcontinents which each of us has to discover and explore is the labyrinth of the dark, the unconscious, the shadow side. Many artists can be helpful to us here, but none more so than Irish artists. Beckett explained the proliferation of poets in this country by suggesting that when you are living on the last ditch in Europe there is nothing else to do but sing. Certainly being on an island makes one aware both of the meagreness of what is our own and the immensity of what is outside. Whatever the reason, the number and quality of Irish artists 'tackling this dark', as Anne Madden called it in an interview in 1997, is proportionately vast.

It is randomly interesting to note that Tom Murphy's first play is called *A Whistle in the Dark* (1961); John McGahern's second novel, *The Dark* (1965); Seamus Heaney's third book of poetry is a *Door into the Dark* (1969), and Seamus Deane's autobiographical memoir is called *Reading in the Dark* (1997). For examining the dark there is nowhere more dedicated than Ireland. Brendan Kennelly has spent most of his artistic lifetime in this element.

> Got a job in the sewers. With
> Helmet gloves rubber clothes flashlamp
> I went down below Dublin
> From Kingsbridge into O'Connell Street,
> Flashin' me lamp in the eyes o' rats
> Diabolical as tomcats. Rats don't like light
> in their eyes.

However, artists are not enough. They are no more than ushers, pointers of the way. Art must be precise and personal at this level and in this dimension in order to introduce us to what is proper to ourselves. But then each one of us has to take up the torch and carry on down our own tunnel to the underworld.

The word 'proper' in my title means 'belonging or relating exclusively or distinctively to'. It comes from the Latin *proprius* meaning 'special' or 'one's own', and it finds its most specific form in the term 'proper name', indicating an individual person. So, my proper name, as opposed to my surname (the one identifying me as one member of a family), is Mark. It is as personal to me as my proper dark. And yet, I do belong to a particular family and I was born in a particular country and so this personal dark has similarities with the one experienced by other Irish people. There is also, according to Jung, a collective unconscious belonging to particular races which makes their darkness more familiar to each other than it would be to an explorer from another tribe.

And no tribe, tongue, people or nation can absolve itself from this essential task or refuse to make this journey, and we have fortunately been provided with most talented sherpas and guides. So we can get help from our own artists even though we are not in any way restricted to these. When I suggest that it is Ireland's role in Europe to be in the forefront of this exploration, I am neither proposing some kind of shadowline chauvinism, nor belittling the efforts of other great European artists.

Indeed, perhaps the greatest of them all, William Shakespeare, has hardly been surpassed in his treatment of this subject. One example is *The Tempest*, reputed to be his last work. The play takes place in the symbolic setting of an island but it represents each one of us in our own intestinal labyrinth. Prospero is both Shakespeare and each one of us in our artistic capacity as ruler of our own island and principle of unity in search of harmony in our lives. The two strange creatures who inhabit the island with Prospero are Ariel and Caliban, the first representing 'spirit', the second representing 'flesh'. Prospero's daughter Miranda represents the new humanity which can come from his climbing into his proper darkness. The famous quotation, 'How beauteous mankind is! O brave new world, that has such people in it,' is hers. But this brave new world is a human world. When asked about Miranda, 'Is she a goddess?' The reply is very definitely, 'Sir, she is mortal.' Shakespeare is telling us that the new humanity, the brave new world, is not achieved by either rejecting or conquering ourselves. We have to free the Ariel in ourselves, the creative spirit, but also we have to assume the Caliban, the monster of the flesh. The whole island was Caliban's by Sycorax his mother until Prospero took it from him. Prospero imprisons him and treats him as a 'poisonous slave, got by the devil himself.' 'Filth as thou art,' Prospero addresses him, 'I have used thee with human care, and lodged thee in mine own cell, till thou didst seek to violate the honour of my child.' Eventually Prospero is led from this condemnatory stance to understand that in order to restore peace to the island, to his own territory, to his own humanity, he has to take a different attitude from what Caliban represents in all of us. 'This thing of darkness I acknowledge mine,' he confesses in the end, 'set Caliban and his companions free – untie the spell.' The play is a description of the journey; the voyage of life, which eventually leads us through the necessary and painful tempest of the title, to the discovery of our own reality within the island of ourselves. The play ends:

> O rejoice
> Beyond a common joy, and set it down
> with gold on lasting pillars. In one voyage
> Did Claribel her husband find at Tunis
> And Ferdinand her brother found a wife
> Where he himself was lost; Prospero his dukedom
> In a poor isle; and all of ourselves
> When no man was his own

3

ARRESTING THE SYMPTOMS OF A SOULLESS SOCIETY

John Lonergan

Two hundred years ago Edmund Burke said, 'If we command our wealth, we shall be rich and free; if our wealth commands us, we are poor indeed.' Ireland has recently become a wealthy society – for some. The challenge now is to stop ourselves becoming a selfish and uncaring one. I would suggest that by far the most important aspect of the conference is the fact that it is taking place at all. Yes, we live in the era of seminars and think-tanks, but they all focus on single issues. There is a singular absence of serious reflection on the whole purpose and meaning of life in holistic terms. How do we manage our new-found prosperity? How do we see our society developing during the next millennium?

Margaret Thatcher once said 'There is no such thing as society. There are individual men and women and there are families.' She was wrong. There is a society and it is us. One of the most negative consequences of that philosophy is that it encourages abdication of responsibility for the direction and well-being of society. – It encourages the mé-féiners, those who close their eyes and ears to what is happening around them and who can, thanks to that philosophy, passively ignore the wrongs and injustices rampant throughout society. We selfishly demand more and more 'rights' whilst continually ignoring our responsibilities. Having become immersed in materialism we have forgotten about our deeper human needs and those of others. Many of us can no longer distinguish between luxuries and necessities. Let us not forget that just one hundred and fifty years ago we experienced the Great Famine when millions of our people died. A shortage of food was not the problem, the problem was the selfish refusal of those who had the food to share it with those who had not. Unfortunately our society is still divided into 'haves' and 'have-nots'. One of the questions we need to address urgently is 'Are the haves of today any more generous and compassionate than their counterparts of one hundred and fifty years ago'? How can we stop for long enough in our mad rush towards total materialism to reflect, to take time out to look into our hearts and souls and to listen to ourselves and to others?

My task today is to identify some of the symptoms of a heartless and soulless society and to suggest how we might arrest them. You will notice that I have taken the liberty of including heartless because I find it impossible to separate it from the soul.

Society begins with the individual but they are not independent of each other. All human beings grow, develop and discover their abilities and self-worth through their interaction with other individuals. Every individual must have a role in life and society in order to become part of it. The process begins with how much respect we give to individuals and how much we appreciate them. No two individuals are the same; each one is unique, but we all share a fundamental desire, whether we realise it or not, a desire to be loved and accepted.

Jean Vanier puts it well: 'Man's primal cry is to be loved'. And the first place the individual looks for love is to the family. The importance of the family unit in Irish society contributed enormously to the quality of life of past generations. Generally, the family provided a supportive, caring and stabilising environment for all its members as well as acting as a strong, rock-solid buffer during difficult and stressful times. The traditional family was the corner-stone of society and families interacted together to form communities which, in turn, became the arena for people to grow in in terms of relating to each other and creating a sense of belonging to something bigger than a group of individuals thrown haphazardly together with no common purpose. There was a real sense of community spirit which was clearly evident in the amount of sharing and caring which took place – the sharing was not confined to worldly goods but involved the sharing of time and talents.

I think it is fair to conclude that in contemporary Ireland the three elements of human infrastructure, the individual, the family and the community at large, are currently experiencing dramatic change and all are in need of urgent attention. Individually we have become self-centred and selfish, giving very little attention to the needs of others. The 'I'm all right' philosophy is very evident. We measure our time in terms of money. Most of us only get involved in an activity if we will gain materially. Individually we have allowed ourselves to become total 'mé féiners'.

The nature of the family in Ireland (and elsewhere) is undergoing a huge upheaval. The traditional, two-parent, child-oriented family is no longer always the norm. Marriage breakdown, separation, divorce and single parents greatly impinge on the stability of the family structure. Again, traditionally, mothers played the central role in unselfishly caring for their families, but the mother's role is also undergoing significant change. Many mothers now work full-time outside the home, some due to economic circumstances, some by choice. Whatever the reasons, women's role within the family has changed, as has the role of the traditional 'breadwinner', the father. As a society I feel we have failed to address our new situation. Many women who do still work full-time in the home are made to feel inadequate and apologetic about it. Whilst our Constitution fully recognises the special status of women in the home, the State has singularly failed to act upon it or to amend it in order to give full recognition to either parent working full-time in the home. We must fully and actively support those who work full-time in the home given that they are the most immediate and important role models of our society, without whom we would be lost.

The number of dysfunctional families is on the increase. Why? Inadequate parenting, unemployment, poverty, addiction, poor housing, ghetto conditions and culture, together with the inability to form and sustain lasting relationships, all contribute to this situation. The family home is also under attack – the cost of housing is putting the purchase of a family home out of the reach of many young people. We are told this is due to the 'free market', or we are told that the Constitution does not allow the State to intervene even if the 'free market' in the area of housing means the blatant exploitation of young people. In the interest of the common good we must intervene and do so urgently. If the Constitution inhibits our intervention, the solution is simple – change it. We must not stand idly by while young people are forced to mortgage their entire lives to bricks and mortar.

We must never assume that just because we are amongst people it follows automatically that there is a sense of belonging. A young first year student at University College Dublin recently told me that he passes by thousands of fellow students every day but he feels totally alone in the college. The human need to relate to other human beings and to have a heart-to-heart talk is a most natural one. It seems to me that the only listening facilities available in modem Ireland are those provided by the professional listeners. It has become one of the fastest expanding industries of this decade. We have psychologists, psychiatrists, counsellors, therapists, group facilitators, radio phone-in shows, etc. Have we become the society of the paid listener? Are the rest of us too busy to listen on a totally human basis'? The professional listener is no substitute for genuine friendship. The sad reality is that when the paid session ends the professional shuts the door and the client is on his own again.

Human beings need to talk and to be listened to – it is not an illness or a problem, it is natural, at all stages of our lives, but is there anybody listening?

The old concept of the local community is also being threatened. We all need to develop a sense of identity and belonging and the local community once provided the platform for this. Are we losing our sense of community? Are we imprisoning ourselves in our own homes and consciously shutting out our neighbours? Indeed, does such a species exist any more? Has the pub become the focal point of our community? Television, video and the internet have replaced interaction with our neighbours. Visitors to the home are made to feel like intruders. As a consequence we have become indifferent to the needs of the weak and inadequate in our community. Nobody knows and nobody cares any more, the philosophy being 'it's not my problem'. Why have we built huge local authority housing estates not only bereft of amenities and facilities, but of professionals? The professional's presence is on a visiting basis only. They all live outside the estates. Have we built colonies of social lepers who are not to be touched by us or us by them?

I must reflect for a few moments and focus on rural Ireland, a very crucial part of our country. Currently, rural Ireland is under attack. Once it too benefited from the 'free market' but now, of course, the same free market has turned its back and the consequences are potentially disastrous. When lambs are being sold for as little as £3 each it is time to take notice. Unless this is rectified the very future of rural Ireland is at risk. What will become of the small farmer in the third millennium? Without a viable income there will be no future. Will we become a nation of ranchers, a replica of modern Europe, and if we do, what are the consequences? We need a national plan to deal with the future of rural Ireland.

Every night in our urban areas many hundreds of people are homeless. As a society, we simply do not care, but even worse is the reaction of people when a statutory body or voluntary agency attempts to respond in a meaningful way – there are strong objections raised and in most instances the best-laid plans are hijacked. How often have we heard the claims of pressure groups that social service facilities would create problems and disruption in their area and the value of property would be reduced? Human needs must not be responded to in such an un-Christian and selfish manner. In addition, many of our socially inadequate are treated as rejects. We have huge numbers of people, young and old, who simply cannot cope on their own. There are those who suffer from addiction, have serious personality and behavioural problems and are incapable of caring for themselves. The easiest response is the 'hand-out', but hand-outs are not the answer. They may cover an immediate crisis but the long-term solution depends on a more tolerant and compassionate society – commodities as difficult to find in contemporary Ireland as gold in the Burren.

It is appropriate at this point to refer to the recent public campaign demanding professional child-care facilities and standards. This is most laudable but it is motivated and directed to meet the needs of just one category of people – mainly working parents. What about all the thousands of young mothers who assume the onerous responsibility of caring for their children without any specific training or support? There is no such thing as rehearsal time for being a parent. Why do we assume that they are not in need of help? Why do we assume that they are all 'qualified' in the skills of child-care? Parenting is a most demanding and skilled vocation. However, we provide little support for young parents, particularly those in our most socially disadvantaged areas. All potential parents, men and women, must be provided with the basic knowledge and expertise to enable them to care for their babies – it is very much in our long-term interests.

The huge expansion of the nursing home industry is another symptom of our soulless society. Of course, nursing homes are often the only option available to provide proper care for our elderly. However, this is not always the case and, regrettably, in all too many instances, it is the only option considered. Nursing homes are often lonely places where many elderly people spend the last years of their lives walking around aimlessly, staring at televisions or at ceilings. Is this what we must look forward to towards the end of our lives? What is it telling us about ourselves? Are we becoming a selfish, uncaring and inhuman society? We live in the 'disposable' age – are our elderly now disposable?

One of the latest demands to hit the public arena is the issue of paying our home-carers. Is this another indication of our materialistic society? Is caring for our own families now to become a business? Those who put other people's needs first by caring for them should be treated in a most supportive and respectful manner by the State. Paying people to care for their own families, except in cases of financial hardship, is wrong, and is an insult to the many thousands of people who care for people simply because they care.

It is appropriate at this juncture to raise the whole issue of the medical treatment of the sick, particularly the elderly. Two issues in particular need highlighting:

1. Why are so many hospital appointments made for the same time – usually 9 o'clock in the morning? We have queues of people waiting around hospitals for hours on end for their '9 o'clock' appointments. Whose needs are being met – wealthy consultants 'or sick patients'?

2. The chances of getting some local GPs to undertake home visits at night or over weekends are nowadays very slim indeed. Time after time one hears of appalling responses by local GPs to urgent calls for medical help. Coping with the frustration of the answering service is an added dimension. The reality for many families is that they can be left for hours on end waiting for a positive response. We are shortly reaching the stage when people will have to be programmed when to get sick. Such cavalier treatment of our sick and elderly is but another symptom of our heartless society.

Our education system is directed totally in favour of the

middle and upper classes in so far that it is producing highly qualified professionals for the workplace and is very much achievement orientated. Success at post-primary level is measured by the points system. We have second-level students (those who can afford it) spending most of their summer holidays doing special courses and grinds aimed at topping up their academic points tally.

Consequently, third-level points are developing into a type of snobbery league. Unfortunately our educational system is contributing to this. Are we all contributing to it by our support of the grinds industry? With such huge pressure on academic achievement it is little wonder that so many of our teenagers are burned out, browned off and unable to cope by the end of their secondary education. Is the high number of suicides within the school-going population a confirmation of this? Regrettably, suicide attracts one of the last remaining social stigmas in Irish society. It is swept under the carpet and we pretend it never occurred. Our hypocrisy knows no end. Finally, our educational system has not only failed miserably to bridge the gap between the social and economic 'haves', and their counterparts, the 'have-nots', but it is sustaining it.

At the coal-face of prison I have a unique opportunity of observing 'justice' in action. I have met so many people who have ended up in prison not because they were criminal or dangerous but because there was no other place to care for them. I think in particular of the many women – young and old – who were totally helpless and inadequate. Every day we have at least five or six seriously mentally disturbed or inadequate men and women in prison. Why do we as a society treat these people in such a callous manner? This year, a middle-aged woman spent twenty-eight days in a padded cell in Mountjoy awaiting transfer to the Central Mental Hospital. She needed medical treatment and care but she had to wait for almost a month before her cry was heard? To really rub salt into her wounds, during her time of crisis she received a criminal conviction for entering a store-room in a city hospital with intent to steal bandages. Enough said.

There are many forms of addiction in modern Ireland. In working-class areas it is usually drugs, alcohol and gambling, while in middle- and upper-class areas it is probably shopping – for themselves. The damage being caused by the widespread use of illicit drugs and alcohol throughout our society requires a national planned approach and huge resources, not mickey-mouse ad-hocery. We must not stand idly by as thousands of our young people are destroyed by drug and alcohol abuse. It is a shame that we can find official funds for all sorts of gimmickry, for example, spending over a quarter of a million pounds on a millennium clock that drowned in the Liffey or subsidising the farce of the Tour de France, but we do not have the will to do something about one of the greatest scourges to afflict us. What are such symptoms telling us about our modern society? We don't appear to care. Are we becoming a self-centred, greedy and heartless lot?

The direct relationship between drugs and crime is well documented. Unfortunately, many of our crime problems are interwoven with our drug problems. Research has indicated that crime flourishes in areas where there are high levels of unemployment, inadequate housing, poor education, under-resourced social and environmental facilities, social stigmatisation, lack of skills, high levels of personal stress and tension – often leading to violence and, above all, feelings of low self-esteem. Why do we continue to sustain such conditions? Imprisonment on its own is not the solution. Prison is not capable of undoing in a short period the damage inflicted over a lifetime. As a society, do we care? Why have we failed to allocate the necessary resources to take these people out of their misery?

Eddie Naughton, writing in the *Irish Times* in 1994 about his drug and crime infested community in the Coombe area of Dublin, wrote as follows: 'A friend of my wife voiced the despair she and others who have addicted children experienced – "Thank God life doesn't go on forever", she said, "There has to be something better than this". Who will rid us all of this and let us live a life?' Only a hypocritical, heartless and soulless society could sleep easy in the midst of such human suffering and despair.

The whole issue of professional and white collar crime is very much in the public domain at present. We have professionals, industrialists and financial institutions all involved in or accused of crime. What is the driving force behind this? Is it greed, human weakness or the absence of moral values'? We certainly have not come to terms with it as we continue to treat this type of crime quite differently from even petty crime. Why?

Creating an acceptable image is high on the priority list of most of our public representatives, industrialists, financial organisations and the consumer industry. Public relations experts are paid huge sums of money to create popular and acceptable public images. Many of the images portrayed are shallow, false or fictitious. This is achieved by 'spinning' the truth and the experts doing the spinning are our latest gurus, the spin doctors. They are paid to put a spin on everything which means that at best they are economical with the truth and at worst they totally misrepresent the real situation. There is something basically wrong with such manipulation and it is not surprising that these falsely created images so often come home to roost and to haunt us. How can we have any degree of public transparency while the professional image-maker has such a prominent role in modern society? There should be no need to put a spin on the truth.

The media has been given the huge responsibility of being society's main watchdog and influencer. In fairness to the media they have been given this role through default, due to the decline in the influence of the Church and of politicians. The main role of the media must continue to be the reporting of the salient facts and to provide responsible comment. The public has a right to be aware of the particular agenda being followed by any particular unit of the media. The media must resist the temptation to create human monsters. A good example is the fifteen-year-old who some years ago was labelled the 'Young General'. This was irresponsible and a serious abuse of power by some of the media. The media too must be open to criticism when it is appropriate and it must ensure that such criticism is heard. But who has the courage to criticise the media? The reality is that most people fear the media as they feel it has the power to destroy them. The media must not use its power as a weapon to destroy people who criticise them.

I want to share a little story told about Pope John XXIII. When he was a Cardinal in Venice he was approached at supper by his secretary and asked, 'When are you going to get rid of this troublesome priest?' The Cardinal picked up his wine glass and asked his secretary 'Who owns this glass?'. The secretary replied 'You do, Eminence'. Then the Cardinal dropped the glass on the floor and it shattered. He again asked the secretary, 'Who owns the glass now?' and the secretary replied 'You do, Eminence'.

The Gospel imperative 'to listen to the enemy's story' is still a great challenge. We are becoming an intolerant and self-righteous people. We instantly condemn and reject those who have offended or sinned and we refuse to hear them. We have developed a hardness of heart which prevents us from empathising and sympathising with others in their hour of need. We demand more and more punitive penalties while we smugly exonerate ourselves from any responsibilities. Do we not have to look at the enmity within ourselves? One would be forgiven for believing that all our 'sinners' have landed on us directly from Mars. The reality is that all our sinners are our own people. We must accept that individually and collectively we have contributed to the ills of our society. We are obliged as Christians not only to listen to the enemy's story but to forgive him. Forgiving one's enemies is still a most basic Christian requirement. Regretfully, the example given recently by the

Catholic Church in this regard is very depressing. It too has coldly distanced itself from its sinners and in many cases totally ostracised individual clergy. I look forward to the day when the Catholic Church will give real example by publicly identifying with its sinners, like Christ did. Church leaders should not be aiming to please the public and the media. They should courageously practise what the Gospel announces. The most appropriate place to begin is by publicly forgiving their priests who have sinned, by identifying with them in their time of need and by openly and actively initiating the process of healing.

I am reminded of the homogenised bottle of milk. It does not matter when you arrive at the breakfast table, you still get your fair share of the cream. Being first to the table is no longer an advantage. It must be the same with our new society, everyone must be treated equally.

My vision for the new millennium is of a society which is caring, compassionate, forgiving and sensitive to the needs of all our people, where rights are balanced with responsibilities and, above all, a society where people's needs come first. A society where everyone's opinion counts and where our wealth is divided fairly.

Currently we are a very fragmented society. I have outlined many of the symptoms of our brokenness. Any society which continues to ignore the human needs of so many of its most vulnerable and weak members is soulless and heartless. At the start of my talk I stated that the most important thing about this weekend was that this conference was taking place at all – a forum of reflection. We are a society divided by self-interest groups who shout at each other but refuse to listen. We have already a structure in place to develop and plan our social and economic policy – the social partners. We now need a much broader based but similarly structured forum to bring about genuine human inclusiveness and togetherness. We really need a forum of reconciliation.

May I end by quoting Nelson Mandela in his statement in the dock in South Africa in 1964:

> I have fought against white domination, and I have fought against black domination. I have cherished the ideal of a democratic and free society in which all persons will live together in harmony and with equal opportunities. It is an ideal which I hope to live for and achieve. But, if needs be, it is an ideal for which I am prepared to die.

A VIEW FROM THE CHAIR

Marie Martin

I was surprised at the feeling of peace I experienced when I took the chair on the first day of the conference. The upturned faces of the huge audience radiated good will and high hopes. I somehow knew they would not be disappointed. It suddenly seemed so right that the conference was being held in this place, at this time, for these people. As I shared these sentiments with the audience, I could see heads nodding in agreement. This was to be 'a conference like no other' as a speaker from the floor was to express it later.

Viewed from the chair, the conference was 'like no other' in many ways. That first day brought together some of the finest speakers it has ever been my privilege to hear, and raised very high expectations – which were subsequently fulfilled – for the second and third day. I was soothed by the serene countenance and soft voice of the first speaker, Sister Thérèse, yet disturbed and challenged by her fearless call to give expression to our contemplative dimension in order to nurture our hungry soul, and by the stark choice she put before us – to live from within and be free, or to live from without and be enslaved. There was something thrilling, too, about her confident claim: 'If you live from within, everything will be different, and I mean EVERYTHING.'

As I looked at the second speaker, Mark Hederman, I saw eyes sparkling with intelligence and a face alive with enthusiasm for his theme. In strong, confident tones he challenged us intellectually, spiritually and emotionally. His plea that we should climb 'into our proper dark', own and acknowledge it, was initially startling and unsettling. I tried to gauge how the audience were reacting and was immediately struck by the quality of their listening. They were paying rapt attention to every word, not always agreeing, sometimes appearing puzzled, sometimes enlightened, sometimes even annoyed, but always fully engaged with the speaker. His vision of a holistic humanity with the dark and the light integrating harmoniously as in an orchestra was described to me later by a delegate as 'consoling, inspiring and liberating'.

The third and final speaker of that exciting first day, John Lonergan, swept over us like a tidal wave. A man of abundant energy and deep compassion, he painted a vivid picture of the soulless society that is modern Ireland and confronted us with our indifference, our complicity and our hypocrisy. With vigour, humour and passion, he swept away our complacency as he aligned himself with prisoners, travelling people and the urban poor whose very addresses imprisoned them more securely than Mountjoy ever could. He had an extraordinary effect on us all. He made us laugh though we felt like crying. He opened our eyes though we secretly preferred our blindness. He tore away the labels that we had so smugly placed on others – and on ourselves. 'I have never seen anybody all bad in prison,' he said, 'or anybody all good outside it.' We gave him a standing ovation.

And then there were the precious periods of silence at the beginning and end of each session. When inviting the audience to enter into this silence, I had suggested that this might 'allow the soul to surface'. From the chair, I had a very strong impression that was exactly what was happening. A healing stillness was created which gave the Spirit freedom to move freely and fruitfully.

The question and answer session was lively and probing and gave me my greatest challenge of the day. With so many hands raised, it was heartbreakingly difficult to choose and to see eagerness give way to disappointment on the faces of so many. That was the only view from the chair that caused me pain that day.

But people do understand. They are forgiving. As I stepped down from the chair after the final session I was embraced by some of those I had disappointed, and, throughout the evening many shared with me their delight in the day. My view from the chair had not been a distorted one. The 'Are We Forgetting Something?' Conference was already proving to be an unforgettable experience. Two more wonderful days would follow and great good would come from it all.

REFLECTION

It is strangely ironic that the world loves power and possessions. You can be very successful in this world, be admired by everyone, have endless possessions, a lovely family, success in your work and have everything the world can give, but behind it all you can be completely lost and miserable. If you have everything the world has to offer you, but you do not have love, then you are the poorest of the poorest of the poor. Every human heart hungers for love. If you do not have the warmth of love in your heart, there is no possibility of real celebration and enjoyment. No matter how hard, competent, self-assured or respected you are, no matter what you think of yourself or what others think of you, the one thing you deeply long for is love. No matter where we are, who we are, or what kind of journey we are on, we all need love.

John O'Donohue (*Anam Chara*)

PART TWO
PEOPLE AND PLACE

4

A SENSE OF PLACE IN THE CELTIC TIGER?

J. J. Lee

The vision that underlay the traditional sense of place was memorably evoked by Eamon De Valera in his radio address on St Patrick's Day 1943, his celebrated 'dream' speech.

> That Ireland which we dreamed of would be the home of a people who valued material wealth only as the basis of right living, of a people who were satisfied with frugal comfort and devoted their lives to the things of the spirit – a land whose countryside would be bright with cosy homesteads, whose fields and villages would be joyous with the sounds of industry, with the romping of sturdy children, the contests of athletic youths and the laughter of comely maidens, whose firesides would be forums for the wisdom of serene old age.

De Valera's vision of what he called 'that ideal Ireland that we would have' is usually invoked nowadays only in mockery of the image of 'comely maidens dancing at the crossroads'. The observant reader will realise Dev never said 'dancing at the crosssroads', and the reiterated quotation merely serves to expose the number of commentators who can't be bothered to read originals and are content with taking their ideas at second hand.

While the derision heaped on the traditional sense of place tells us something about current fashion, all we need note for our present purposes is that, however distant the ideal might have been from reality, it was probably widely shared at the time. And it was shared by many who did not subscribe to Mr De Valera's party politics. Michael Collins and Richard Mulcahy expressed very similar aspirations at the founding of the state. Nor did these necessarily differ from many Home Rule aspirations. Dan Mulhall, in his fascinating forthcoming work on Ireland at the turn of the century, quotes Michael MacDonagh, a leading Home Rule journalist, writing in 1900 of his hopes for Ireland in the new century:

> What I should like ... as a Home Ruler, is the cabins of Ireland full of contentment and quiet happiness, the country retaining its pastoral characteristics, its touch of perpetual spring, ever young and fresh and bright and reposeful, a land of sweet thoughts and quiet breathings, the home of happy agricultural communities tilling their fields and tending their flocks and herds and the towns, few and far apart with a quiet but prosperous trade. This I hope is the good fortune that time has in store for Ireland.

These images of the good society, their cadences verging on the biblical, were suffused with a sense of place, redolent of rooted people with rooted values. But however attractive they may have found their images of the ideal, they were all vitiated by a fatal flaw. They had no grasp of economic reality. The sense of place could not provide either economic or emotional sustenance strong enough to keep the thirty thousand or so emigrants a year, virtually year in year out, from leaving not only their own place, but their own country.

De Valera acknowledged that, in prevailing conditions 'for many the pursuit of the material is a necessity', because they lacked the minimum required to 'make the best use' of their talents. But he also insisted that 'our material resources are sufficient for a population much larger than we have at present if we consider their use with a due appreciation of their value in a right philosophy of life'. That could only imply a very wide gap indeed, given the continuing emigration, between the actual behaviour of the Irish people and Dev's idea of how they ought to behave. And his address contained not a solitary hint as to how the country could get from the real to the ideal. The implication was that it depended not on an economic revolution, but on a moral one – on nothing less than a change in national character, not to say in human nature. As to how that was to be effected, he had no proposals. That is a legitimate and decisive criticism. But it is a criticism of the means suggested, or rather not suggested, for achieving the ideal, rather than of the ideal itself.

Before expressing a view on the ideal, let us first be sure that we know what exactly it was. For it has to be purged of the archaism of the De Valera lexicon – his vocabulary was, after all, that of one of the last of the great Victorians – and translated into language more familiar today. So let us look at what De Valera really meant in terms intelligible a half century later.

'A land whose countryside would be bright with cosy homesteads' meant a well-populated country, with the population broadly distributed and the people enjoying good housing conditions. It also implied the ideal of family independence, where no family need be dependent on any other for its basic needs, and would therefore not be obliged to show deference to any other because it couldn't afford to risk retaliation from stronger players on the market.

'Fields and villages joyous with the sounds of industry' meant full employment throughout the country. Moreover it was to be quality employment, satisfying rather than soul-destroying work. In so far as he meant by industry not only activity, but 'industry' in the narrower sense, he was expressing his frequently stated preference for decentralised industry over large factories or urban concentrations.

'The romping of sturdy children' meant that children should be healthy, and have the opportunity to enjoy themselves as children, instead of being forced into premature adulthood by peer pressure or advertising campaigns, seeking to reduce children, as they would succeed in reducing so many adults, to mere objects of mass market calculation.

'The contests of athletic youths and the laughter of comely maidens' meant that sport should be a central part of young lives, even if the role allotted to the 'maidens' be a more passive one than would nowadays seem appropriate, widely accepted though this was at the time.

'Whose firesides would be forums for the wisdom of serene old age' meant that the elderly should be listened to carefully, their views treated with respect, enabled to live out their latter days in their own homes, living and dying with dignity. More broadly, they should be cherished as integral members of the community, not as surplus to requirements, having inconsiderately survived beyond their proper span, a drag on sprightlier age groups who resented having to lay votive offerings before any deity except Narcissus.

De Valera's model emphasised the essential links between the generations as he identified his ideal for the dependent ages in society – childhood, youth and old age. Giving was as important as taking, service as important as wealth. It was a society in which rights were balanced by responsibilities, in which adults of materially productive years acknowledged non-material obligations both to those who came before and to those who were coming after, the generations woven together into a seamless social fabric.

Many family, social and community relationships at the time bore a broad similarity to the ideal, hideously though some deviated from it. For there could be hatred as well as love, cruelty as well as kindness, calculating opportunism as well as instinctive generosity, within the family, much less outside it. The likelihood is that the balance was heavily positive, although the nature of the memoir market naturally puts a premium on the negative, in much the same way that bad news drives out good news in the media. The old proverb, 'Ar scath a chéile a mhaireann na daoine' still described much of not only the sentiment, but the reality, of Irish life, in which a substantial flow of emigrants' remittances continued to testify to a sense of family obligation.

Even in 1943, however, there was one glaring contrast between the De Valera vision and reality, one that could not be changed by any appeal to human nature or even by a transformation of character. The sense of place his vision invoked was purely rural. It had no place for urban Ireland at all. Of course the country was then much more rural than today. Even so, this still left about half the population living in places other than 'fields and villages', even if many of the places officially described as urban – places with more than two thousand inhabitants – were still quite rural in character. And it was inevitable that the urban proportion would grow. His sole reference to the existence of an urban Ireland came in a quotation from Thomas Davis, to the effect that 'our cities must be stately with sculpture, pictures and buildings'. How this was to happen, however, remains singularly obscure in Dev's delineation of his ideal Ireland.

This Ireland had no place for 'the town I loved so well'. It was therefore doomed, at least in its literal version, simply because it swam against the tide of twentieth-century history in the industrialising world. (Incidentally, its attractions in the real world for the sundered Protestant brethren of either the Shankill or the Malone Road may be imagined.) However the world of the internet and of information technology may transform living conditions in coming times, however grotesque our current style of urbanisation may come to appear to later centuries – for the idea of herding people into often hideously ugly city centres and soulless suburbs, with television acting as the tranquilliser, precisely to spirit one away in imagination from the reality of the emptiness of so much of urban place, may well come to seem a bizarre way of arranging the use of space – nevertheless in 1943 the thrust of economic development made the ideal enunciated by De Valera simply impossible of attainment.

Not only that. The actual policies pursued by Mr De Valera's own government promoted urbanisation. It was the same De

Valera who appointed his most energetic minister, Sean Lemass, to the Department of Industry and Commerce, with a mission to industrialise – even if Dev's idea of industrialisation excluded heavy urbanisation, as he envisaged local factories scattered around the country. It was inevitable that urbanisation would intensify. What was not inevitable was the form it would take, so much at variance with the European and North American norm – though not with some Developing World experience.

Who says urbanisation in Ireland says Dublinisation. The most salient fact of Irish urbanisation since independence has been the growth of Dublin, with the Greater Dublin Area accounting for nearly 40 per cent of the population in 1997 compared with less than 15 per cent at the founding of the state in 1922. Moreover, this growth has followed directly from state policy. When De Valera specifically included a clause in his 1937 Constitution to the effect that both the parliament and the President must be based in Dublin, unless the Oireachtas decided expressly to the contrary, he was merely recognising the existing reality – but he was certainly making no effort to change it. The growth of state employment itself, and of directly related activity, has been the biggest single factor in the expansion of Dublin. The growth of the civil service. the centralisation of the headquarters of over 90 per cent of state-sponsored companies in Dublin, irrespective of the location of their actual activity, the virtually total centralisation of state media, as well as of the lobbying industry, in the metropolis, has been the prime factor driving the relative growth of Dublin.

As so little economic development has occurred independent of state support, directly or indirectly, anywhere in the country, this disproportionate concentration on Dublin by the biggest single employer in the country, the state, has ensured that almost all the internal migration movement has been in a one-way direction to Dublin.

The disproportionate location of higher-level educational

institutions in Dublin has further reinforced this thrust. Given the relative size of Dublin it may seem quite natural that three of the seven universities in the state, University College, Dublin, Trinity College, Dublin and Dublin City University, should be located there, with a fourth, Maynooth, on the outskirts. Between them they account for about three-fifths of all university students. When the Dublin Institute of Technology, the biggest single educational institution in the country, achieves university status in the fairly near future, about 80 per cent of university places will be in Dublin.

This is quite the converse of general European and North American experience, where no capital city accounts for so heavy a concentration and where many of the most renowned universities are located away from the capitals. In the Irish case, the consequences are particularly important. Precisely because migration is almost entirely one way, a disproportionate number of the brightest young people are already psychologically attuned not only to leaving home, but to heading for Dublin. And this tendency is actually intensifying as the total number of university places expands dramatically, with far more young people now, happily, gaining access to opportunities too long denied earlier generations. But the wider implications are left unconsidered. Given the close relationship now established between the location of universities and the location of high quality industry, the implications for job creation at the upper end of the scale are fairly clear.

In the current Irish situation, Dublin largely plays the role of the metropolitan power towards the rest of the country. This is not a formal colonial relationship, of course, but it has many of the same characteristics. Fintan O'Toole, in an article in the *Irish Times* of 30 October 1998, captured the essence of much of it. 'The truth is that rural Ireland no longer exists. Since the arrival of television, the motor car and the multinational company there are really only three kinds of places in Ireland – cities, an extended suburbia of commuters and farmers, and depopulated areas where almost no one lives by farming alone.' Whatever element of exaggeration some might deem this to contain, it undoubtedly puts its finger on some of the main consequences of recent social change. What exactly do they imply?

'Cities', as we have seen, is largely a euphemism for Dublin, With nearly 40 per cent of the population in the Greater Dublin Area, compared with only 7 per cent in the next major conurbation, the Greater Cork Area, the disparity between the size of the first and second cities is wider than in any country in Europe or North America. In demographic terms, whoever says city effectively says Dublin.

In social and cultural terms, the ratio, if these things could be measured precisely, would be likely to be far greater, with Dublin-based publicists and policy-makers accounting for perhaps 90 per cent of power and influence. Dublin is overwhelmingly the media capital. When we refer to television we mean essentially, where Irish television is concerned, Dublin television. There is some chance of hearing voices from outside Dublin on public affairs programmes, because the rest of the country still sends politicians to Dublin. Commentators, however, will be almost entirely Dublin-based. This is no sin. As individuals they can be highly accomplished. But the lack of geographical no less than social diversity means that there is little variety in the predominant perspectives represented. The presence of so much journalistic and academic talent ensures a ready supply of articulate commentators, but with a rather narrow range of intellectual positions, so that little real debate occurs.

This Dublin media base, perhaps inevitably at the current stage of intellectual development, serves in large measure as an enclave for imported thought, which it then distributes throughout the country as the most advanced fruits of the human mind, given that so many commentators still equate advanced thought with whatever the current fashion across the Irish Sea happens to be. It is already programmed to filter out any disagreeable line which may conflict with its commitment to allegedly liberal political correctness. Ardently though it proclaims itself liberal, still exulting in its escape from what it sees as traditional claustrophobic Catholic conservatism, it is the reverse of liberal in the classical sense, in its reluctance to evaluate the evidence for all sides of arguments with an open mind.

Ireland has in large measure moved from the argument from authority from the pulpit in the Church to the argument from authority from the pulpit in the television room. The message has changed, but the personality types delivering it have often remained the same, with, if anything, fashionable media thought often more intolerant than that from which it purported to have emancipated the natives. Ireland beyond Dublin is then the passive recipient of much metropolitan admonition and exposition. It rarely hears its own voice, except in local radio and local papers. Local radio has made a difference, but it would be interesting to inquire how far the local media itself serves as an enclave for the distribution of Dublin-transmitted thought, or are capable of thinking independently on the basis of local circumstances.

It is not, of course, that one would wish to reject thought simply because it is 'made in Dublin', or, more accurately, is distributed through Dublin. Much of it may be of high value. The issue is whether it should be regurgitated unquestioningly or accepted only after critical scrutiny.

In case my position be mistaken for, or caricatured as, a presentation hostile to Dublin, it should be stressed that this inequality of access to a Dublin-based media discriminates not only against the population outside Dublin, but against the vast majority of Dubliners as well, who have no more chance of access than the residents of geographically remote areas. Exclusion from a media which constantly preaches inclusiveness does not begin somewhere down the country. It begins within Dublin itself. When we refer to Dublin we don't mean a representative cross-section of Dubliners. We mean the handful of people whose names and faces recur constantly as media Dublin and, by extension, media Ireland. Fintan O'Toole's description evokes this dependency of the *de facto* colony on the metropolis in a material sense, much less a mental one, very well.

If Dev's dream Ireland had no place for cities, the Ireland described by Fintan O'Toole has little for country or even towns. Towns as well as villages have now been sucked into the city vortex, meaning the Dublin vortex. This is an entity – it can hardly be called a society – based on exclusion. It is defined in terms of the exclusion of those who fail to conform to the model of the geographically mobile, who have no need of a sense of place. People exist only as producers and consumers. There is only one generation involved, there being no place for the uneconomic. It is a one generational Ireland, it is an economy, not a society. It is therefore virtually the polar opposite to the dream Ireland of De Valera, which was far more a society than an economy.

It is therefore logical that just as Dev's time horizon was virtual eternity, as he traced his ideal Ireland from childhood through youth to old age, a virtually static society wending down from generation to generation in a series of endlessly repetitive cycles, so the Ireland O'Toole describes exists only in the here and now, the commuter consumed by the needs of the present as he or she hastens to desk or studio. The generation that lives for the moment has no time to even ponder what will happen itself when it reaches old age if its children take their cue from itself and become as consumed with itself as the parents now reputedly are.

There is, happily, an irony here. If the real 'traditional' Ireland had a certain sense of community, it was no stranger to economic calculation. A sense of place by no means ensured sentiments of spontaneous generosity. Place offered no guarantee of protection against exploitation, even if it set certain limits on the possibilities much of the time. Few had a more sensitively developed sense of place than the gombeen man. Traditional Ireland could be coarser than its image in certain respects. On the other hand, even a people who allegedly set their clock bv the sound of the cash register can still indulge sentiments of solidarity with family or neighbour. In both cases behaviour can diverge for better or worse from the dominant principles of public discourse, whether familial or individual.

But what is certainly true is that the objective challenge of generational solidarity has become more daunting with the passing of time. With both parents in many cases working outside the home, the caring function – whether for the elderly or for the children – has increasingly to be transferred to institutions. One might think that the sharp fall in completed family size in the past twenty years would allow more care for dependents. But that has to be, in turn, balanced against the pressures of outside work on parents, with the consequent rationing of time for young and old. In addition, the demands on parents have greatly increased through the rise in children's expectations fostered by the advertising culture, when the children of poorer and of more affluent parents are exposed equally to the sales talk. It has probably never been so hard to be a child, and never so hard to be a parent, as it is today. In the case of single *parents*, whose numbers have spiralled in recent years, and who will rarely dispose of comfortable incomes, the pressures must be more intense still.

At the other end of the generational scale, medical and nutritional advances mean that more and more people live longer, leading to all sorts of potential complications, depending on precise family circumstances, especially in urban situations. Some elderly people have been fortunate to find happiness in old people's homes run by nuns and nursing orders. But the number of these carers is declining, and others can be guided by more mercenary motives. How people choose to treat their elderly is one of the surest guides to the level of civilisation, and how the generation now entering into old age fares will tell us much – maybe too much – about ourselves. In any case, changes in relations between the generations, which have, for the most part, occurred silently and invisibly, have been among the strongest influences loosening the concept of the home, which is itself a powerful component of a sense of place.

Children and the elderly get in the way of economic man and woman. They are generally physically and psychologically less mobile, appreciating some sense of stability in their relationships, wanting to be able to trust others, needing to relate to people rather than things, generally less obsessed with using relationships for personal gain.

Must they then be excluded from the world view of the Celtic Tiger? Are they to be victims of a Tiger that has no sense of place? Are the complaints one hears about the selfishness of the brave new Ireland or, depending on your values, the eulogies to its belated modernisation, Europeanisation, globalisation, its finally catching up with cosmopolitan values, an Ireland the media and the multinationals made, all justified? Has the Ireland of the Tiger succeeded in breeding a rootless people, for better or worse according to taste?

Hopes or fears to that effect continue to be eloquently expressed by concerned observers. As I happen to believe that a certain sense of place has an important role to play in sustaining the vitality and the decencies of a civil society, I'll concentrate on the fears rather than the hopes inspired by the sense of its impending dissolution. It is perception of this levelling influence that lies at the root of the doubts voiced about the allegedly pernicious, or at least potentially pernicious, consequences of the Celtic Tiger. Niall O'Dowd, writing in the *Irish Voice* of 3 February 1999, assembled a number of observations stimulated by Sister Thérèse Murphy's *Irish Times* article, which asked why so many are 'harshly disillusioned' by the results of prosperity. Eddie Holt, an incisive television critic, responded that 'there is a me, me, me, attitude – very prevalent in Ireland now. People are in love with the Celtic Tiger and the notion of it is pumped out all the time. It infects the media very seriously. There's no such thing as history or a sense of place, it's all about grab what you can, when you can right now.'

Holt is no lone voice. The new 'Ireland of the Welcomes', according to Kathy Sheridan, another *Irish Times* journalist (23 January 1999), 'is over-priced, under-serviced and distinctly unfriendly'. Michael O'Loughlin, back in Ireland after twenty years away, observed 'on the one hand, a burgeoning underclass racked by drugs, gangsterism and poverty, and on the other, spectacular wealth, vulgarity and indifference... in the New Ireland, money is the morality, the spirituality, the Meca' (26 January 1999). Niall O'Dowd himself observed that 'If you take a stroll down Grafton Street, Dublin's main shopping thoroughfare, it is like any American mall nowadays with the number of international stores completely dominant. In the rush to conform to the latest fashions, Irish kids are indistinguishable from an American high school class. None of the traditional individualism of the Irish is immediately apparent. You could be in a Long Island shopping mall for all the diversity or Irish sourced products you will find.'

There is a huge irony lurking in all of this, The fashionable criticism of De Valera's Ireland has precisely been its allegedly stultifying conformity, a belief proclaimed as an axiom of ideological faith, a revealed truth no less. Now conformity seems to be breaking out all over again – and to be rampant among those who pride themselves on their individualism!

This is not, however, the whole truth. Niall O'Dowd himself asks 'Is this necessarily a bad thing?' His answer is that 'There should he a certain sadness, I think. The traditional image in

America of an Ireland of thatched cottages and peasants dancing at crossroads is justifiably laughed at now in the new Ireland, yet the Irish seem ever more anxious to recreate themselves as some ersatz Atlantic offshoot of America with all the worst elements of this culture mixed in … how they handle this burst of prosperity is every bit as important as how they handled adversity in the past. The jury is still out, I think.'

'How they handle it' depends partly on how place is incorporated into the value system. That in turn depends partly, we have suggested, on the future of the family in Ireland, which is now increasingly contested. Much will revolve on how far families provide secure moorings for the emotional stability of their members, or how far they become simply one more institution to be functionally exploited, to be embraced or discarded as individual opportunism dictates. There has always been an element of this in most families. The question is where the balance will be struck. Media morality is almost entirely on the side of subordination of family feeling to individual interest. There is certainly room for debate on family relationships. But the ideology of the media virtually precludes reasoned debate.

Given my belief that a certain sense of place can play a civilising role in the modern world, it may seen perverse of me to welcome, indeed to rejoice in the Celtic Tiger, however long it may flourish. This is not for a moment to deny the gross injustices that scar our society, the lack of equality of opportunity, the lack of equality of access to resources, including educational and media resources, that so influence life chances, or the, ravages caused by drugs or drink, or the abuse of the weak by the strong in so many ways. But none of these has been caused by the Tiger. Some may have been exacerbated by it, but they all existed in greater or lesser degree before it. It is we, after all, who decide what to do with the surpluses generated by the Tiger. If we blame the Tiger for whatever we wish to condemn we are in fact blaming ourselves.

It can certainly be the case that sudden exposure to wealth, for countries no less than individuals, can lead to much unbalanced behaviour. And our economy has grown at an extraordinary rate. After a good, but not spectacular, performance between 1987 and 1992, it has grown by over 50 per cent since 1993, or an increase in five to six years that equalled the increase in the first forty years of independence. But whatever misuse may be made of the gains, I rejoice not only because of the material price, but even more the psychological price Ireland paid for economic failure.

The bottom line of historical reality was that for generations Ireland could not create the jobs to keep her people at home, or to give them the choice of whether to go or stay. It is only ten years since we were losing more than thirty thousand people a year, or had real unemployment levels here at home verging on 20 per cent. The bulk of emigrants probably did better by leaving than by staying, and presumably felt generally happier, whatever the occasional intensity of nostalgia for home. But it was a forced march for them. There was no dignity about it. It left much loneliness behind. It is no doubt true that emigration in the age of the airplane and telephone does not involve so final a sense of break as in earlier generations. Nevertheless involuntary emigration at any time proclaims the primacy of market values rather than human ones in the organisation of society. For those who reject that value system, and refuse to internalise the value system of the power players in the economy, a sense of place is one weapon against the levelling principles of economic determinism.

How easily we can forget. It is only a decade since a Tanaiste told a New York audience that emigration was a way of life because, 'after all, we cannot all live on a small island'. There wasn't space for barely three and a half million of us in the Republic, one of the most sparsely populated countries in Europe? What an extraordinarily defeatist sentiment from anybody, much less as courageous and ebullient a personality as Brian Lenihan. And that sense of defeatism had spilled over into so many areas of Irish life as to penetrate to the very marrow of our character – the willingness to be satisfied with second best, bluntly expressed by an internationally successful Irish businessman, Denis Brosnan, defining *Irishness* in 1986 as 'the capacity of the Irish to accept and/or deliver standards which appal many of us... it is the antithesis of quality'.

One can blame 'history' far too much for many things that are more the product of the present than of the past. But when you have had battered into you, sometimes physically, more persistently psychologically, the idea of the inherent inferiority of everything of yours compared with everything of your conquerors, of your culture, of your language, of everything that makes you you, generation after generation, century after century, then inevitably you internalise much of that instruction. Your self-image becomes heavily influenced by it. Your self-respect is fatally undermined by it.

In the modern world the most effective antidote to it is economic success. That has become a crucial component of perceptions of performance – and because our self-image is significantly influenced by what others think, we not having yet acquired sufficient self-confidence to be indifferent to it, that matters greatly at this juncture. The quality of economic performance therefore far transcends the purely economic. It is possible that having been blamed for many things unfairly throughout history (as well as some things fairly) we are now reaping excessive credit for some things we don't deserve. Much (though by no means all) of the spring in the Tiger's step is due, after all, to multinational companies, who account for a disproportionate amount of our exports. But who are we to look a gift Tiger in the mouth?

The Tiger, whatever his genetic provenance, is delivering. What are we to do with the proceeds? There is a clear conflict of interest between, on the one hand, those who worship at the altar of the Tiger, red in tooth and claw, who hold that those in a position to do so should rip off whatever they can and the devil take the hindmost, where the individual is the measure of all things, and one's sole duty is to oneself and, on the other hand, those who believe in some idea of society. For the first set of believers, place has no sense whatever, except in a purely functional and opportunistic way. For the second, place has a significant sense, though how it relates to other values needs to be carefully worked out.

This is all the more necessary in that the 'traditional' sense of place cannot survive without adaptation. If a sense of place is to survive, other than as nostalgia, it must change. It would have to change for simple practical reasons even if it weren't under ideological threat at all. Young people today travel far more than ever before. A century ago, even half a century ago, it was still quite common for emigrants never to have travelled more than a few miles from their birthplace until the time to emigrate came. That is no longer the way. Young people will now travel regularly even if they live at home

Some of this follows inexorably from the changing nature of work. Farming, where workplace and home were effectively identical, still the biggest single occupation in 1943, has dwindled, and will continue to dwindle, as a source of employment. Even those who worked outside the home and farm, urban or rural, generally lived close to their work. It is only a slight exaggeration to say that we are all commuters. Nor is the concept of a job for life anything like as pervasive now as it was then. Young people, in particular, at least in the private sector, think nothing of changing jobs several times when the market is buoyant, even if this rarely involves migration out of Dublin.

It may be that developments in information technology will in due course revolutionise the relationship between home and work, but that will not happen overnight.

One cannot expect that a sense of place will come nearly as naturally to future generations as to past ones, even in rural areas. Or at least not the same sense of place. Even with past generations it could change over time. When the GAA began – and the GAA has been one of the great bastions of a sense of place throughout the country, as have other sports in particular parts – the parish featured relatively more prominently than the county, counties being represented by the county champions in intercounty competition. While the parish has by no means faded into oblivion, it is the county that now takes centre stage at national level. Nationalism itself, of course, came in due course to transcend, even while it incorporated, a local sense of place.

In an age of rapid change, and of more frequent questioning of identities, a sense of place has now to be cultivated, in country as well as town and city. Given the pressure on families, even fairly close-knit ones, in the urban world in particular, it is now institutions outside the family which bear much of the burden of providing bonding relationships, especially for young people. Schools, sports clubs, youth clubs, provide some sense of belonging. Where they fail to do so, either in reinforcement of, or as substitute for, the family, the camaraderie of the street and of gangs fills the void. A sense of place in this context must include a sense of urban place, above all of Dublin place. Not all suburbs need be soulless. It will be a matter of choice for most people, but it will only happen if sufficient people care, and if the institutional structures necessary to foster it, both state and voluntary, can be put into place. A psychic sense of place will become more important than simply a physical one, even though the physical will inform the psychic. Nor is this necessarily a bad thing. When place is defined too narrowly, it can be more claustrophobic than comforting. While a large proportion of the whinge in Irish literature can be taken with a substantial grain of salt, there is no doubt that it captures a sense of confinement that many could find emotionally crippling.

How successful a sense of place will prove to be in providing a sense of security, a sense of belonging, amidst the swirling currents of the new millennium, depends on which concept of society proves most attractive. If there is no such thing as society, in the celebrated phrase attributed to Mrs Thatcher, and as is inherent in the ideology of extreme individualism, there can be no sense of place.

The issue then, for those who subscribe to some sense of society, is how does one reconcile the principle of rootless individualism with a sense of social solidarity. That poses a profound challenge for all inherited values of any solidarity type, and for the institutions that embody them, in an age of globalisation. For what is globalisation? It is not, as an optimistic version might like to delude itself, a benign blending of all that is best in all the cultures of the world, a ceaseless harmonious epiphany of all that tugs at the heartstrings of humanity, the ultimate unity in diversity of a world finally elevated to its universal plane.

However appealing that prospect in the realm of food – who could be so crass as not to relish the variety of cuisine on offer in Greenwich Village – that is not the essence of globalisation, Irish style, as currently in process. For globalisation, far from being a blending, is an imposition of the strongest material and media culture on the weakest. This simply means that it is a euphemism for economic, social and cultural Americanisation, or rather for Americanisation as represented and exported by a particular segment of American mass media. This by no means reflects the totality of American society, a society of immense ethnic, cultural and linguistic diversity, that diversity which forms an essential constituent of American character and American greatness. Ironically, a power whose greatness is built on diversity is now threatening to reduce the world to uniformity in the name of diversity.

The very first requiem of a vigorous indigenous response is

that there be sufficient worthwhile jobs at home to persuade young people to stay in Ireland and, where they so wish, close to home. That means having a thriving economy, and prosperity widely diffused, both within Dublin itself and throughout the country. How is that to be achieved? It has defied even those who genuinely desired it for so long that one must accept there is no easy or simple way of doing it. It is possible that in an age of IT the strictly economic obstacles to diffused location of jobs will decline. But there is huge psychological pressure to keep clustering in the Dublin region.

The biggest hope for diffused prosperity is diffused third-level education. The location of economic activity, and therefore of potential community vitality, is increasingly influenced by access to good quality higher education. We have seen how relatively well Dublin is catered for by university institutions. There is always the possibility that educating young people locally will simply amount to educating them out of their localities if the jobs are not provided locally. But the young people are likely to go anyway in that event, whereas there is some chance of holding many of them if they can be provided with satisfying jobs in the vicinity.

The role of the Institutes of Technology, located around the country, could be crucial here, if it can be reconceptualised further. They are one of the best things ever to happen to education in Ireland, if only because of their location. Not only are they major employers in their own right, but they create further job potential in the vicinity. But they should be seen not only as centres of technical advance for their commodities, but as centres of thought. They ought to be at the cutting edge of thinking about the future of their areas – and ask not only what are they educating for, but *where* are they educating for. The only reason for them being where they are, after all, is the importance of place. Every Institute ought to have a vibrant heritage section – and not as an act of piety, but as a centre of lively thought on the future of the region in the context of where it has come from, where it is, and where it could go. Their thinking in this respect ought in turn, to fold into national thought, which should be energised from the ground up as well as from the top down.

It would be ironic if the major centres of education throughout much of Ireland were to act simply as unofficial conduits of the thought of others, as equivalents of the mercantile enclaves which imperial powers established in colonies whose job it was essentially to exploit the colony for the imperial power rather than develop anything indigenous, and whose imports often served to destroy local initiative rather than enhance it.

One of the central challenges for regional educational institutions is to develop a capacity for independent critical thought, which will clinically evaluate media thought, whether metropolitan or directly imported. The question has to be constantly posed for any vibrant society, as for any vibrant individual: Where do they get their ideas? Why do they choose one perspective rather than another, how far have they thought through their position, or how far are they puppets of media mechanisms of indoctrination? That is why opportunity for debate, for discussion, for challenging the consensus should be an integral part of the vitality of a region. Information technology is transforming the potential of distance education, but it is essential that local institutions retain control over the content, and aren't simply expected to regurgitate whatever the centralised fashion of the moment may be. They have to be education centres, not indoctrination centres. Parity of place has to be a core value of any genuinely democratic, pluralistic society – and how far are we from that, even within Dublin, much less between Dublin and the country? There can be no genuinely inclusive society without parity of access to the media, national as well as local, of people having a right to speak for themselves, rather than constantly being spoken for, without more direct democracy, if one will.

In De Valera's day, independence was conferred on the individual/family by the possession of property. Now education has become the main route to independence, and is increasingly the key to property, except at the levels of luck or politics that attach to high finance, the world of sport and mass entertainment. But for the big majority, it is education that opens opportunities for independent activity, and protects them from being, at the mercy of a single employer or source of indoctrination.

A sense of place implies belief in an inclusive society, where the weak are cherished as much as the strong. How far it will be sustained in the Ireland now emerging depends partly on factors beyond our control in an age of globalisation. But it also depends largely, like so many other things, on how we choose to respond to globalisation. It means influencing, if not capturing, the commanding heights of opinion formation. It means a conscious attempt to build institutional structures, especially educational ones, that keep open the possibility of viable communities outside the metropolis and, equally importantly, within it. It means two-way movement of people rather than simply one way, with all roads leading to Dublin, in the interests of both the country in general and the quality of life in Dublin itself.

It means operationalising all the fashionable, but frequently fraudulent, rhetoric of inclusiveness and pluralism. It means equality of access to the public media – equality by place, and by age, as well as by gender, instead of confinement to the charmed circles of a couple of square miles, and to the privileged age and professional groups. That may require an effective quota system, given that 'merit' has little meaning in this context. It means much more democracy in a media which constantly invokes the principle, but rarely practises the reality.

Whether that will happen I don't know, But it certainly won't happen by itself. The market – for ideas even more than products – is rigged against it. That is why initiatives of the type being launched here by Fr Harry Bohan are so potentially important. There is a long struggle ahead – a twenty-year march through the institutions – if the drift is to be reversed, and Ireland is to become a genuinely inclusive, pluralistic society; words that trip so lightly off our lips and which are so often belied by our behaviour and to whose achievement a balanced sense of place can make an important contribution.

5

TOWARDS A NEW IRELAND

Tom McGurk

Such has been the rate of change in technology in the last two decades that one can hardly imagine the extent of the change in the next two. By say 2018 – only 18 years into the millennium – can we imagine where the technological revolution will leave us? In our homes, as a result of the growth of satellite and digital television, we may be able to receive anything up to 200 channels. Through the internet, we will shop, talk to each other, exchange information and as is apparently the case recently, fall in love and marry. What is certain is that we will be in an age whereby the power of what I call popular culture will be immense and probably overwhelming. Will we be able to see the wood for the forest of aerials?

What is the role and function of the media in relation to popular culture? What is popular culture and what is it that culture seeks to popularise? In particular I am talking about the media in the new millennium.

Consumerism is now beginning to represent itself in pernicious ways in the media. The bible of the advertisers is a concept called 'attention span'. It works at two levels. One, how long is the average span of attention of the average person? And, two, since advertising on television is by definition very short, how is it most effectively used?

So we arrive at the concept of the message – both liminal and subliminal. This has become so effective for advertising that now it has passed into politics and into democratic society. Before any politician these days faces the reality of the live interview, he has himself produced. In this he is treated exactly like a product – as if he is for sale. Toothpaste, washing powder, tar, politicians – it's all exactly the same. The same people sell both – image consultant, hairdresser, speech-writer. The politician, like a packet of washing powder, is given an image, a snazzy presentation and a short-attention-span message. 'X is good for you', 'X washes white', 'Vote X into office'.

What effect does this have on the media? Is their response conditioned by the same approach? This is the route of tabloidism. In their attempt to sell their product, they live by the same rules. 'Attention span, message, image', the song says – the thinking person's lager lout. And the link between the two, between the politician as product and the newspaper as product, is the sound-bite. What determines the sound-bite? Our old friends – the attention span, image, snappy, memorable phrase, etc.

So what is going on here? Where in all of this is the sovereignty of the fact? This information in a democratic society, is not Mrs Thatcher's oxygen of publicity, but the oxygen of democracy. Is it not underscored by critical analysis, veracity, socio-economic sub-text, but instead, is a series of facts in quotes, chosen by the rules of product placement, in thrall, not to the demands of objective analysis but to the requirements of consumerism. In other words, have facts and information become products to sell? Furthermore, if those who now own the most popular organs of opinion disagree with the political message, how can they respond? By analysis? No! By argument? No! By negative advertising. The *Sun* says, 'Rubbish!', The *Irish Sun* says 'Get Your Knickers In A Twist'. But where does all this leave the conduct of public affairs by the media in a democratic society? Is this politics by information, leading to legislation, or politics by lager lout? Tabloidism very quickly builds its own constituency. In the last twenty years it has become a cultural voice in British life. The advertising AB1s, as they are called, are the constituencies, living on the edge of consumerism, mortgaged to the hilt, or not at all, with their preferences, with xenophobia, and deep anger.

Tony Blair learnt the lesson very well. Forget about white-collar, blue-collar or no-collar, British society is composed of two classes and two classes only. 'Broadsheet readers' and 'tabloid readers'. 'BBC 2 and Channel 4 watchers' or 'Sky 1, 2, 3, 4, 5, 6, 7, 8 watchers and Sky Sport watchers'. They are the new divisions in society. Class, economic divisions, expressed as consumerist divisions. Ask any media analyst what the New Labour voter eats, drinks, drives, and he can tell you.

And now in Ireland a new tabloid generation is emerging. Who are they? What do they look like? They wear Manchester United tracksuits. They spend Sundays in pubs watching Sky soccer. They are, increasingly, young. Sales of the *Sun* are principally to the younger generation. These people belong to a very different Ireland, to the one you belong to. They are principally located in working-class areas. They no longer have the protection of association with the great defining things of Irish life – extended family, sense of place, parish, community, Church. These are people who live between different wants of consumerism in a growing society and their external society. So what we are now faced with is a huge dilemma in the consumer society: the sovereignty of the fact against the sovereignty of the consumer's right to choose. If he chooses fiction or factual entertainment, has he that right? Have we reached the stage where freedom of speech has the right to enslave itself? The concept of popular culture also has wider, less recognisable hallmarks and in ways more implications for what goes as standards in our society.

One day last week, I was somewhat astonished to see a photograph of Bono and The Edge and some other pop singer whose name I do not know, standing in front of a huge billboard for Amnesty International in O'Connell street in Dublin. They were then joined by Michelle Smith, the controversial and suspended triple Olympic gold medal-winning swimmer. The caption read something to the effect that the rock stars were gathering to help Amnesty gather one million signatures in

Ireland for a worldwide petition in support of human rights. The petition will be presented to the United Nations in December on the fiftieth anniversary of its founding. According to the *Irish Times* report, Bono said 'One of the greatest problems in the world is the cynical idea that the world can't be changed and that politics and economics are too complicated to deal with. But with Amnesty it's simple. You can write a postcard and make a gigantic difference to the life of someone who is in jail or suffering human rights abuse'. And he added that Amnesty was, and I quote him, 'a cool club to be in'.

So what is going on here? What are the values implicit in this scenario? What is this 'cool club' all about? More importantly from the perspective of what I'm talking about, is this popular culture and if it is, what is it saying? Even more importantly, on whose behalf is it all operating? At one level the whole business is so graciously and offensively self-serving, the implicit and quite breathless cheek of turning a matter like human rights into a photo opportunity for those of celebrity status is deeply offensive and outrageously cynical. Is there no longer any relationship between the desired achievements and the method of achievement? Between the shadow and the substance is there no longer any moral high ground? Equally, what are we to make of the mentality of those who believe that somehow the universal demands for human rights can be sated by the simple stratagem of getting rock stars to sign gigantic postcards for delivery to that unstoppable gravy-train called the UN? I think that if we all take one step back from this scenario, draw breath for a moment and consider what is going on, then we can begin to see the subtext of popular culture in all its unmissable and irredeemable cynicism. What is actually going on here is an act not of political intent at all but an act of consumerism. This is a transaction and everybody is buying and selling. Amnesty is buying publicity and good will and selling a simple stratagem for our consciences about human rights violations. The rock stars are buying a popular, feel-good little number, a 'cool club' as Bono called it, and they're selling themselves, their records, their posters. their T-shirts. This is the outrageous spectacle of brand-imaging on the backs of God-knows-what atrocities worldwide. And what are we buying and selling? We are buying the wisdom of a popular culture that dictates that if you generate enough publicity, with the appropriate icons of modern consumerist success – in this case, singers who can flog their records, in remarkable quantities – then you can move the Generals in Indonesia, the politicians in Serbia, and, indeed, the bankers of the IMF, in whose name, human rights across the Developing World are in such short supply. But what we are selling is immensely important. We are selling out our genuine concern for human rights by being party to this stratagem. We are giving our pennies to the black babies of our age by the simple stratagem of signing our name.

No, don't get me wrong, I am not suggesting for a moment that popular conscience is not a force for change. It certainly is. In 1989, while working as a foreign correspondent in Eastern Germany, I watched in fascination as the Soviet Empire collapsed by dint of the fact that people loaded their families, their blankets and their pots and pans into their Trabant motorcars and simply drove across the Iron Curtain into democratic Europe. Not a shot was fired, the tanks stayed locked up all day, only the traffic policemen were busy. The German part of the Soviet Empire collapsed when its comrade citizens simply got up and walked away. Ironically, one of the most powerful forces in that change was the inability of the old Eastern regimes to stop its citizens receiving television signals from our side of the wall. The longer they sat in their workers' apartments surrounded by their regulation furniture in front of their black-and-white television sets and watched the myth that the popular culture of our television screens dresses up our society to be, the more determined they were to join us. Indeed, at this moment, in a curious way it was the advertisers in their open-plan offices rather than the generals in their concrete nuclear bunkers, who brought the whole edifice collapsing down. These consumers on the other side of the wall, without a penny to spend, incidentally, believed it all. They really believed, that just across the bricks and mortar was a world where Panadol killed pain, where Daz washed all our stains away and where all was possible with interest-free credit and no payments until April of next year. There was one extraordinary moment that I will never forget when the bizarre value system of our consumer society confounded these people.

I remember they went down to the border in their ancient Trabants, their Volkswagens and their Mercedes, with their families, their pots and pans and their blankets. They went to the Red Cross tents, got their voucher for somewhere to stay. They drove down the road to be waved down by German car dealers, who were fascinated by these 1931 and 1933 Mercedes E-classes and long-disappeared Opels and, there and then, on the road, these East German citizens were offered a new BMW for this 1936 Mercedes E-class which was held together with wire. The drivers from East Germany could not believe what was going on. They had had this 'bloody thing' for fifty years, holding it together with wire, without parts, and the first thing they wanted to do when they got into democratic Europe was to get rid of it. They couldn't believe that West Germans in sharp suits wanted to buy these motor cars. What conceivable use could these motor cars have? Of course they were classic cars and had great value. That was a strange moment for these people in understanding the values of our consumerist society.

I should imagine that now, some eight to nine years later, those same people have a quite different view of the veracity of popular culture, of the image and the message of modern consumerism. Yet, in a quite remarkable parallel, we too on this side of the long-gone wall, are now facing a similar crisis of identity as we approach the millennium. As the new consumerism and media age that lies just ahead of us masses its forces and, as the people who control the spread of news and information in our society, and the people who own the consumerist empires, become one and the same people, we face a potentially extraordinary society. Once upon a time when I began working in television, we used to joke that our job was merely filling in the spaces between the advertisements. That is no longer a joke. It is becoming increasingly the case. Particularly with an empire like Rupert Murdoch's and, increasingly, others, we find that the people who own the goods that they are flogging during the commercial breaks are also the people who own the programming that is broadcast between these commercial breaks. Like the rock stars seizing on human rights as a feel-good hinterland to sell their personalities, to project an image of their caring and decency against the context of human rights abuse, so also the emperors of the new television age seek the imprimatur of caring and goodness for their commercial intentions. Editorial then, ceases to be independent and sovereign in its own context. And, importantly, that context is the strand of public opinion and knowledge that links it to the functioning of our democratic society. Instead it is becoming yet another weapon in the consumerist's armoury. This functions in two quite separate ways. One is by producing popular programming in the context of fiction and light entertainment and the other is by attempting to popularise non-fictional concerns. In this the former is the typical diet of say TV 3 or Sky One in Ireland, 'junk food' bought cheap in the USA and the southern hemisphere and rebroadcast here. It's a sort of verbal chewing-gum and, while I am sure it serves to stunt all sorts of development, at least you can tell the depth of it, by feeling the width. Nor does it attempt to masquerade as anything other than popular entertainment. But the second proposition is a much more serious matter. It is becoming increasingly powerful and I believe it represents a serious threat to journalism and, by extension, to how any democratic society sees itself. This is the business of attempting to popularise fact by various stratagems. To the commercial television bosses, I suppose it all smacks of Bono's instinct that 'it's a cool club to belong to'.

And it is a cool club. There's real life crime, real life problems of life and death, and even, if they can get their hands on it, real life news and current affairs. Take real life crime and watch the growing profusion of police or cop programmes, as they are called. This involves the simple stratagem of putting a video crew in the back of a patrolling police car and shooting from the hip. Here we are in the front line of crime prevention, riding stagecoach with the sheriffs of our modern cities. Other people's problems always make great television: from the distance and safety of our living-rooms we can satisfy our prurience and our feelings of being up there on the moral high ground. Even the policemen become actors in all of this, stars in their own right, and the criminals too. The world of crime becomes the world of showbiz. Most nauseating about this conception of programming are the presumptions implicit in it. The easy divisions between right and wrong. Certain questions are never asked, the agenda is simplistic, banal and entertaining. What causes crime? Why do the police always seem to be working poor neighbourhoods? Are the people whose doors the TV crews step through behind the police ever asked their permission? Do they have any rights of privacy if prime time television decides to do a slow pan around their untidy bedroom, their grubby bathroom? As their children wail in the background they often seem to me to be curiously quiescent, humbled, shamed. Are you surprised? One moment they are alone in their living-rooms smoking a joint or something – and its always the lowest level of crime that these programmes track – and next thing the door comes in and they are on national television. So what have we here? Crime programming, – programming that might attempt to ask the real questions any society has to ask about crime? Programming that might ask questions about offenders, about the system of justice? Hardly.

What we have here is low-life showbiz, with the public as unpaid performers and with crime being addressed not as a source of concern for society but as a source of entertainment. This is what the new bosses of television mean by info-tainment. I repeat – information entertainment. Take their next growing area – personal relations. In the US, the Fox Corporation, owned by Rupert Murdoch, hit on the wonderful and cheap stratagem of filling the afternoon television studios with what are described as trailer park folk. Trailer park folk are America's poorest. And so we have shows like *Ricki Lake, Gerry Springer, Geraldo*, etc.

In most circumstances, what the participants, or the victims, to put it more accurately, say is actually scripted. And so we sit back in the name of human relations, under the guise of investigating sexuality, family relationships, domestic lives, etc. and watch the truly horrible scene. The audiences are encouraged to shout and roar like a bullfight audience, and participants often come to blows. All this modern television circus needs is some Emperor to give the thumbs up or the thumbs down. And, indeed, they are there too, up in the administration offices watching the viewing figures.

Some years ago in the US such was the problem of getting big audiences for news programming, particularly since they occupied important time slots, that American television chiefs called in the advertisers to help. What can you expect from a pig except a grunt? Of course they came up with the truly revolutionary notion of asking the people what they wanted to see on the news. Now why had nobody never thought of that before? It's the ratings – stupid! And so the telephone pollsters began and the folk with the clip-boards set off from main street. We want happy news, they were told, more gossip, more news about celebs, more sport. We want sexy newsreaders. We want sexy weather forecasters. We want entertainment, we want the news to be, what does TV3 call it? – 'News with the Human Touch'. And it worked. Well, the ratings went up and he who pays the piper calls the tune. Info-tainment has toppled its greatest rival. The huge edifice of journalistic standards went hurtling over. Now we were all in show biz. Wheee!

Those who, in recent weeks, have watched in astonishment the soap opera which the Clinton Presidency has become, may now begin to understand. Put two thousand journalists in the White House Press Corps, let Bill and Monica loose, cue Linda Tripp, and who needs *Dallas* or *Neighbours*? *Washington Behind Closed Doors* never looked like this. And so we have the Congress of the United States attempting to impeach the President. But why has he remained so popular in the opinion polls if Congress want to impeach him? It's the ratings – idiot! You can't fire the star of the movie, the hero never dies in the good old Hollywood way of things! The White House would be Dallas without JR. Indeed, who killed JR? Should he be slain? Who will slay Bill Clinton? The man with the phone poll and the ratings card. The man with his finger on the nation's funny-bone.

Now there are many of you who will say this could never happen here. Only in America. The programme to parody Jackie Healy-Rea will never be made. But I'm afraid Bono's cool club grows by the hour. There is the television ratings process called contamination. What Murdoch began with Fox has now spread to all the networks in order to keep their ratings. And sleaze, gossip, sex and dirt are popular. The viewers want bread and circuses. If in 2018, were Sky Digital and TV3 digital to start capturing the vast part of the Irish audience, what would and what could RTÉ do? Were the same to happen in the UK, if say, ITV took its trousers down, would the BBC not follow? And what then? Tell the people they can't have what they like? Didn't Stalin try that one and lost? And remember our friends across the wall in East Germany? What did they do when they were told to watch only home-produced communist programmes? Give me my remote control, I'm still king in my living-room.

In any society, journalists are the hewers of information and carriers of fact. Some may imagine they are in showbiz, but don't mind that. A hack is a labourer at the bottom of the democratic heap. A coolie for democracy, in that, it is his job to dig out the nuggets of information and facts on which the public exercises its democratic franchise. In the triumvirate of society, the hack is the man who supplies the punter with the information in the ballot box, in deciding against which politician they put their X. The hack should have no axe to grind, either on behalf of consumerism or popularity. In fact he should always say the unpopular thing and always ask the unpopular question. He should be by nature a permanent pain in the arse in all situations. Among the exotic fragrances of consumerist Valhalla, he should have sclerosis and stinking feet. And most have.

But above all he needs protection, he needs a society which begins to care as much about what masquerades as popular culture as it cares about its wildlife or its trees or its schools or its education. Don't try to save your green environment and forget what comes out at your children from your television screen. And hacks are powerless in the face of something like Murdochisation because, among other things, he pays them too much money for their principles. The control of television and newspapers is in your hands. You elect those who regulate it. If in 2018, you have a media where topless women do the weather forecast and where hacks are such celebrities, that they too will be famous enough to stand in front of human rights posters, to encourage signatures for human rights, or better weather, or cheaper drink, or nude bathing, or whatever, that will be your failure. We hacks have mortgages, ulcers, overdrafts and Uncle Rupert has a huge expense account. We don't want to leave you, but... .

High above us, in the sky, as we approach the millennium, the electronic dustbins of Mr Murdoch's satellite army are massing, and within months tens of new digital channels will be on stream. In the shops in Ireland the worst of the yellow end of Fleet Street, repackaged as the *Irish Sun*, God bless the mark, are cheaper and cheaper. Tomorrow the *News of the World* will only be 30p. You will not understand what a frail plant an Irish media, in the services of Irish democracy and society, is, until you see it disappear. You will miss us, I think. That is, if and when we're gone, and that is too, if you will know then who you are any more. We tell you who you are – not what you should buy. We tell you what's wrong with us – not what's sort of cute about us. We tell you the world is full of sharks and liars – not full of AB1s and AB2s. We tell you how it is, not how we would like you to think it is. We are not selling you anything, we have nothing to sell you. We are not salesmen or entertainers or celebs or even rock stars. We are cynical, mostly underpaid nosy parkers. You probably don't even like us and that's the way it should be. We think we are an essential species but we know we are not a protected one. Mind us, protect us, lock up your drinks cabinet and your daughters if you like , but remember, come the millennium, in the new media world – in the Valhalla of commercial telly and info-tainment, we will not be wanted any more. The big question is, will you still want us?

6

FROM BOOM TO BUST AND BACK

David McWilliams

Economic wealth – nurture or nature?

How come Switzerland is so rich? Is there something superhuman about the Swiss? In contrast, how come Russia never made it? From Catherine the Great, Peter the Great, Lenin, Stalin and Gorbachov, the Russians have made a dog's dinner of creating sustainable economic wealth. Why?

Consider Venice, a city-state that was the wealthiest place on earth a few hundred years ago. Now it is nothing but a tourist attraction. Why did its medieval dynamism disappear? Will the vibrant city-states of the late twentieth century, Singapore and Hong Kong, go the same way? Why did Britain blow it so spectacularly this century? Why did the Asian Tigers collapse so startlingly in the autumn of 1997?

History can help us answer some of these questions but we have to go back to the starting-line, to a time when income disparities between countries and within societies were negligible.

At the beginning of this millennium most people in the world received the same income. The difference between Ireland and England was minimal as was the difference between Ireland and Algeria or Russia.

Dissemination of innovation (spreading of knowledge)

By 1200, China rather than Europe looked more likely to emerge as the economic giant. It had more people and was more technologically advanced than Europe. Inventions were proliferating in China and it appeared to be at the cutting edge of technology. However, two seemingly innocuous inventions mastered and developed by the Europeans at the time explain why it was the Europeans who encroached on China's shores in 1500 and not the other way around.

Spectacles were invented in Venice around 1350 and they prolonged an artisan's working life by about 200 per cent. They also allowed finer workmanship which in turn led to mechanised industry. Finer machines led to bits of machines fitting together: mechanisation.

Clocks, developed in Switzerland and the Lombardy plains, were in widespread use before the Renaissance. Clocks allow people to time things and thus measure productivity. With fine machines to make things and clocks to regulate and measure production, Europeans began to mass-produce.

China had both these inventions but rulers did not allow their dissemination down to the artisan class. The dictatorial relationship between peasants and rulers ensured the artisan class remained very small. Mechanised Europe began to pull away.

History tells us invention is not enough. Inventions need to be harnessed via the dissemination of information. If countries want to get rich, inventions and their use must be passed down through the population. Therefore, lesson number one is that adaptability to new ideas and a level of economic freedom make it worth while for people to adopt new technologies.

Enquiry and dissent

A century or so later, when the mechanised Europeans took to the high seas in search of trading ideas, the Portuguese and Spaniards led the charge. However, things started to go wrong almost as soon as gold from the New World reached Iberian shores. Both empires went to Latin America, robbed gold, came home and spent the proceeds. It was a bit like a lottery winner blowing the proceeds in double quick time. How did this happen?

Interestingly, coincident with the discovery of the New World came the expulsion of non-Christians during the Spanish

Inquisition. The Jewish and Moorish populations were forced to flee Iberia. However, the age of discovery had been driven largely by the Jewish and Arab populations. These were the astrologers, map-makers and tacticians who facilitated both the Portuguese and Spanish navigational feats of the 1500s. They were the ones continually questioning and trading. Unfortunately, they were replaced by the monotheocratic dogma of Catholicism which existed in a feudal system of landowners and peasants with few or no property rights.

Having been miles ahead of the posse, these societies began to go into reverse. My own feeling is that this stemmed from a lack of dispassionate enquiry and a failure to oppose dogma. Dogma leads to economic stagnation. Lesson number two is that a society will only remain dynamic if it allows dissent. It is no surprise that contemporary dictatorships tend to come unstuck due to economic underperformance.

Dynamism

Elsewhere, while the Iberians were sinking gradually under the weight of theocratic superstition and the excess of bingeing on New World booty, Holland and England were surging ahead. Holland was one of the smallest countries in Europe in the 1600s and 1700s, yet by the 1770s it was the richest country in Europe. Although the Dutch were without resources, they became wealthy through trade, commerce and enquiry. For the Dutch, the Reformation did change things but then again, maybe the Dutch changed the Reformation. In addition, the lowlands were the main recipients of the dynamic Jews fleeing persecution in Spain. There does seem to be a direct linear connection between questioning by the private individual (whether religious or otherwise), property rights and economic wealth. Lesson number three is that size is not everything. A small dynamic country making the most of its talents and infusing its workforce with new ideas will outflank the competition.

Copying and catch-up

Then in the 1800s, England took over the baton of industrial leader, spurred on by amazing innovation in production techniques. Again, the English example is much like the Dutch, both rather small countries when compared to France and yet both powered ahead, while France languished economically.

Then when the game appeared to be over and England's Empire appeared all-dominant, it began to lose its economic clout and Germany, the US and later Japan took over. Lesson four is that others learn very quickly and catch up even quicker.

Fast-forward to recent years when it was thought that the various Asian Tigers were going to take over the world, yet by the end of 1997 they were all but bankrupt. And so the cycle moves on. History tells us that economics is one large cycle where countries get rich and are then overtaken by others. Industries fall in and out of favour and there is no golden rule for prolonged prosperity. However, irreverence, opportunism, dispassionate questioning, intellectual freedom and property rights do help. Size is not important and small may not only be beautiful but profitable too. Because harnessing ideas can be more important than innovation itself, countries can, contrary to popular belief, plagiarise their way to wealth. The crucial point is embracing technological change and not being afraid to recognise when certain industries have had their day and it is time to move on.

More history – the Americas

Latin America and North America in the 1600s and 1700s can be viewed as being a bit like an economic specimen jar where the theories expounded above can be tested. In both parts of the Continent, Europeans arrived with the crucial weapons of steel, guns, germs and horses which enabled them to win the key battle of the civilisations (Europeans versus natives) hands down.

The Spaniards were very happy for the British and Dutch to go to New York because they felt that there was nothing of any value up there. In contrast, Mexico had gold and silver. In 1700 Mexico was much richer than North America. There were native slaves in abundance, mines and huge spaces for farming. How come, given the much more favourable starting point, did North America became so rich and Latin America so poor?

Much can be traced to the systems which were imposed. Latin America adopted the Spanish system of lords, overlords and peasants which was failing in Europe. In North America, the Calvinists introduced a more egalitarian system which generated a questioning society, and this questioning society generated growth.

With property rights came responsibility, while in Latin America feudal kleptocracy ruled the day. The peasants had no incentive to innovate because the landlords simply robbed from them.

Most importantly, in terms of the flow of ideas and the use of innovation, immigration had a dramatic effect on the pace of growth. Wave after wave of European immigrants invigorated North America. The key was labour (and lots of it) plus the ownership of property rights. In Latin America, immigration slowed dramatically after the initial Spanish plantations and, as the Spaniards rarely encouraged women to emigrate in significant numbers, a macho culture developed where military and masculine prowess predominated. (The descendants of these adventurers belonged to the military juntas which ruled the Continent until recently.) Wars never have a positive effect on economic growth because even though they may prompt a spurt of innovation and production, they cost a lot of money and leave both sides bankrupt. The succession of pointless 'border' skirmishes in Latin America simply sapped the resources of the countries involved.

Only in Argentina was there some brief semblance of economic clarity. From 1918 to 1928 Argentina was the sixth richest country in the world. In 1991 it was a basket case. What happened?

In the last two decades of the nineteenth century, Argentina experienced mass immigration which, as it had done in North America, drove the economy. This harnessed the resources in Argentina and a combination of enterprising immigrants and rich resources propelled it forward. The country soared in the global growth league. Although hard hit by the global depression of the 1930s, there was every reason to believe that a good performance in the 1950s could be expected. Then, with Juan Peron and his atavistic policies, there came a halt to the immigration of all except the most unsavoury Europeans and a nationalisation programme which cobbled property rights. The economy went into freefall for close to four decades.

The American example tells us that the keys to economic growth are people, property rights and relative intellectual freedom. If the people are robbed of their economic freedom they will become docile; likewise, a country with economic freedom but without people will simply run out of steam.

Reasons for wealth – The four phases

While the lessons from history tell us that the key condition is freedom, both intellectual and economic, they also suggest that economic development occurs in phases. At each phase, more adaptable, flexible people come in and add something special which renders their products more sought after than their neighbour's. In economic jargon this is known as 'terms of trade'. I prefer to call it 'pricing power'. Countries move through different phases of growth and as they do so, each phase has more pricing power (i.e. it can charge more for its product) than the last one. There appear to be four distinct phases of economic growth.

1. *The land phase* refers to a stage when owning land was a huge plus. Feudal societies were based on this, as were great land empires such as Russia's. Certain agricultural economies are still based on this phase and even in parts of Western economies the agricultural sectors are still there. The age of

land and landlords is ultimately the least profitable as we go into the twenty-first century.

2. ***The labour phase*** is where most developed economies were in the early part of this century, when cheap labour generated the perspiration to drive economies forward. Many developing economies such as India, China, South Africa and Brazil are still in this phase. Ireland was in this stage in the 1960s until Sean Lemass, realising that we had labour but no capital, changed the tax system to enable us to attract foreign capital (multinationals) to jump-start the country into the capital phase.

3. ***The capital phase*** is where the introduction of capital, either financial or physical, pushes the economy ahead. The US in this century is a great ewxample of this. From 1900 to today each surge in the US has been driven by capital accessibility such as railways, electricity, telecommunications, etc.

4. **The enterprise phase** is where capital is fused with enterprise. This gives us phenomena like branding, marketing and advertising as well as Internet, multimedia commerce and real pricing power.

Therefore, countries which manage to get to the fourth stage tend to find that people will pay more for their goods than countries at the first stage. A great example of this is the price people are prepared to pay for Adidas sportswear in 1999 and the price they are prepared to pay for food.

At the moment, Adidas (an enterprise phase product) can charge almost whatever it likes for its products because of advertising and branding, whereas farmers are faced with consistent falls in the price of beef (a land phase product). Thus countries which export beef see a fall in their income and countries that own the rights to Adidas see a rise in their income. Within countries the same process is going on. Farmers in Ireland have to sell even more beef simply to pay for the fashionable sports shoes their own teenagers want to buy.

Therefore, the phase in the economic cycle is crucial. The demarcation lines between these phases are becoming increasingly blurred for individual countries but the approach best explains why some countries get rich and some stay poor. The economic cycle which sees countries going from one phase to another is either accelerated or retarded by the general politico-economic environment prevailing in the country over several decades. This economic cycle differs from the business cycle in the length of time covered; we are talking decades rather than years. The 'normal' business cycle, on the other hand, measures the time between a recession, recovery, boom, slowdown and back to recession again; normally this is a matter of years. This mini-cycle occurs at various repeated intervals

From Tiger to Tortoise
Lessons in globalisation

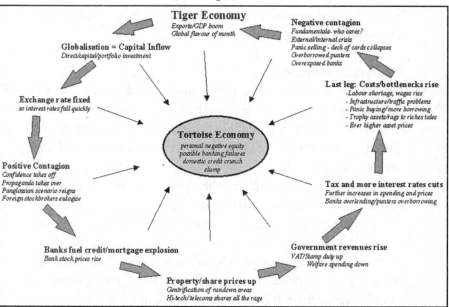

during the long-term economic cycle. In contrast, the boom and bust cycle occurs at the top of the business cycle when everything seems to be going so well.

Booms and busts: A brief history and a few lessons

Ireland has managed to get to the final phase in certain important industries. We have also had a drawn out business cycle. Our last slowdown was a short-lived affair in the early 1990s and was not particularly traumatic. Thus the economy is in the seventh year of the upswing.

Let's look at what I see is an inevitable boom to bust cycle. The boom and bust cycle differs from the long-term business cycle outlined above in that we are now only concerned with the final upswing and the initial downturn.

Economic history is so littered by boom to bust stories that it is difficult to know where to start. When punters begin to pay over the odds for a certain type of asset, this triggers a boom to bust cycle. In Ireland today this asset is property. We have the least populated country in Europe with the fastest growing land prices. This does not make economic sense.

The typical evolution

The boom is usually caused by some sort of positive shock coming from outside. In our case I believe the decline in interest rates from 1993-96 from double to single figures was crucial, as indeed were urban renewal schemes, particularly in Dublin, which made it very tax efficient for savers to move into property. The second stage is euphoria, when prices rise and speculation begins to build both for buyers and sellers.

The third stage is gearing, when people begin to borrow against 'estimated' rather than 'realised' increases in their property prices. We then go to mania, where people get involved because their neighbours are involved. Savers, who otherwise would never speculate, hop on the bandwagon.

The next stage is the bubble, where prices soar to such an extent that the crash becomes an accident waiting to happen. This will come to pass by savvy sellers getting out now, leaving the unsophisticated buyer with an asset which looks slightly overvalued. I call this penultimate phase the stage of financial distress. This is where investors know that they've made a mistake but are hoping to get out before everyone else. Prices level off.

Very quickly everyone realises that the emperor has no clothes and that their apartments are not worth the £200,000 they paid for them. Everyone panics. We then move into the wonderfully titled (in German of course) final *Türschlusspanik* (door-shut-panic) where everyone bolts before the door ultimately closes.

We have seen this type of process in the UK housing market in 1989, the Boston market (the so-called 'condo craze') in 1987, the Scandinavian market 1990-92, the Japanese housing market in 1992 and the Asian Tigers in 1997/98.

Chart 1 outlines how a similar chain of events could transpire in Ireland. We have the Tiger economy which everyone eulogises about. This attracts capital flows because everyone wants a slice of the action. Interest rates come down very, very quickly. Punters start buying houses (boom). People begin to believe their own propaganda. The 'buy a house you can't go wrong' approach to investment predominates (euphoria).

Banks gets in on the action and start lending people money hand over fist. The Government, flush with tax revenue, decides to cut taxes in the next budget (gearing).

People borrow even more and begin to live astride a debtor's bubble. The final phase (where I think we now are) moves us into the real nonsense stage (bubble). Too many cars appear, followed by jams. Bottlenecks emerge. Wages rise in certain sectors and asset prices go even higher. Asia was in this stage fifteen months ago when people began to question the real virility of the Tigers (financial distress).

Just when everyone is having a great time and the party is in full swing, the global recession which has been building hits us. The lights go out (*Türschlusspanik*).

If that happens and I think it will, we could be in for a terrifying crash here. In the event of a crash, people will look to the emasculated Central Bank of Ireland to act. But the central bank will have decommissioned all its economic weapons to the European Central Bank and so it will be powerless.

Against this background, a crash of the same magnitude as seen in the United Kingdom and Boston in the late 1980s and Scandinavia in the early 1990s is probable.

After the storm, where next?

• If we have a crash, the labour market will suffer first. Many of our new service industries – restaurants, bars, etc. – are based on feelgood factors encouraging people to spend. If this were to change in any way, many jobs in this vibrant sector could be lost. Emigration, our traditional safety value, would rise.

• If house prices crash, negative equity is likely to be a common feature. This is made more probable by the difference between the average house price in Dublin (circa £120,000) and the average wage (circa £15,000) and the predominance of 90 per cent plus mortgages. The difference between both can only be sustained by rising house prices. If prices fall, many people will be in houses which will sell for less than their mortgages.

• It is possible that one of the banks in Ireland will fail. Every crisis of this nature has led to a banking crisis. This is why Germans, French and Americans own most major UK banks. The reason is that the UK banks performed so poorly in the 1990s – post crash – they were sold for a song.

• In this type of environment, the national budget surplus will quickly turn to deficit as revenues fall and spending rises. If the Swedish example is anything to go by, a deficit of 6 per cent or 7 per cent of GDP is not inconceivable.

• Consequently, we could move from being the darlings to being the dunces of the EU very quickly. We would break the stability pact (which states that the budget deficit cannot fall below 3 per cent of GDP) and we could revert to getting our wrists slapped in Europe.

After the storm – planning for the future
Like all economies, the Irish economy will survive a crash, maybe a little bruised, but intact all the same. The goal then is to look forward to the year 2020. Listed below are a few pointers which skim the surface of the debate on reorienting the economy.

• History indicates that savers remain prosperous; spenders blow it. Therefore, a slightly less cavalier approach will go a long way post crash.

• The single most important asset we have is people and to this end, our immigration laws should be loosened immediately. There is no economic case against increased immigration; all historical evidence suggests that immigrants boost growth.

• One of the most successful countries in the 1990s is Israel, where the population expanded by 28 percent in one year. These immigrants injected new dynamism into the economy, driving it forward. Immigration offers new knowledge, flexibility and dynamism. We should open our doors immediately. History tells us that economies that work are flexible, adaptable, embrace change and embrace people.

• Similarly, there should be no compulsory pension age.

Compulsory retirement at sixty-five is nonsense. It makes sense if you spend your entire life down a coal mine and so can't dig at sixty-five because you are frail. But if you are spending your entire life at a desk, why should anyone retire? Our work force should include people as diverse as an Irish-speaking eighty-year-old and an Albanian twenty-year-old.

• Contrary to what the European Commission is telling us now, we should keep as many tricks up our sleeve as we can. We should keep our preferential tax system and try, where possible, to use it aggressively. In tandem, the government should continue to cut corporation tax.

• In terms of industrial policy, you don't need to build computer factories for large established firms. Instead of giving a large grant for 400 immediate jobs, maybe someone should be thinking about longer-term indigenous industry. 'Technology Greenhouses', where the government leases land and facilities to entrepreneurs, could be the answer to maintaining a software industry here.

Economic history tells us both how economies succeed and how hubris can trip up even the most successful of these. Busts nearly always follow booms. History also helps us to recognise when the lights are going from green to amber and ultimately red. The evidence surveyed implies that it would be wise for us in Ireland to take precautions now against such a probability.

7

IS IT POSSIBLE TO MANAGE THE FUTURE OR HOW MANY 'N's ARE THERE IN MILLENNIUM?

Professor John Drew

Where will you celebrate the millennium? With whom will you celebrate it? Most important of all, just what will you celebrate? How would you describe an ideal day in your life in the year 2000? Given a magic wand what changes would you now wave into your business, social and personal life? If we define clearly what we want, there is a much better chance of obtaining it! Look at these three circles of our lives:

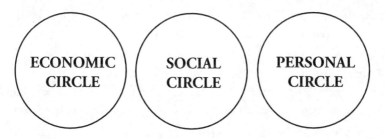

During this lecture I would ask you to reflect on them and on your answers to the three questions I have put to you.

The millennium is a time of great opportunity for our planet. It is also a time of considerable danger. A new year gives cause for reflection, a hundred years even more so. A millennium is something altogether different, especially as it falls by chance (although Jung would call it synchronicity) in the middle of three or four decades of the most profound change our planet has ever witnessed.

As good and bad millennium fever begins to grip us, it is comforting to find that Jung forecast this watershed some forty years ago in *Man and his Future.* Even further back, the Calendar Act of the British Parliament of 1750 was concerned with the year 2000. Pope Gregory XIII identified the year 2000 as a leap year in his Papal Bull *Inter Gravissimus* of 24 February 1582. Would that some of our computer experts in the middle of the twentieth century had given more thought to the problem. The move from 1999 to 2000 by computer clocks is a world crisis, but hopefully not a disaster as embedded microchips in weapons, in nuclear power plants, in off-shore oil rigs and in aircraft control systems fail to recognise the millennium and crash. I have followed with surprise and bewilderment the failure of governments and organisations to assess the implications of the problem early enough, mainly because individuals cannot believe that such a minor sounding problem could become such a major issue.

However, we can be optimistic about new beginnings as we approach the millennium. Opportunities are opening up in a world which is becoming global economically. Worldwide and co-ordinated concerns are leading to action about the environment. Higher standards of living and a better quality of life are issues influencing a society which wants and needs to live in small units, reaching back emotionally and, perhaps, intuitively, to the small towns and villages, where we lived until the Industrial Revolution changed everything.

But the greatest opportunity we now have in our western civilisation is to work on the reawakening of the inner dimension to our lives which for many has withered away or lain dormant since the Enlightenment of the eighteenth century. We have explored our outer world during the second millennium; I believe we shall explore our inner world during the third.

You will notice that I rarely use the words 'spiritual or scientific'. The reason for this is that my theme is very much about connecting our inner selves to our everyday lives and the words we choose to do this are important. I am involved in the personal development of managers. Managers are often seeking permission to talk and learn about the softer subjects of management – of personal destiny, of reawakening, of ethical responsibility, of creativity and innovation, as well as the harder subjects of financial control and accounting, of marketing and production.

We are just beginning in our more enlightened corporations to understand the concept of artists in residence in City of London finance houses, of poets who talk with top management at the Boeing Corporation. Coaches, counsellors and mentors are understood or sometimes misunderstood in a growing number of organisations. We place heavy emphasis on communications, but less emphasis on the words we use in communicating. When putting embryonic, delicate and perhaps important ideas to general audiences, the messages can be drowned by the words we use to convey them. How often I am approached by therapists, by psychologists, by a wide spectrum of workers concerned with the soulful side of life and asked how they can get their ideas and approaches over to general audiences among whom there are many, they suspect (not without reason), who are seeking permission to air their longing for more support and guidance as they feel their way hesitatingly towards a better understanding of their inner lives.

'How can we better communicate what we can do?' they ask. I remind them of the story of the German army surgeon who needed to amputate the leg of an Indian prisoner during the First World War. Neither of them spoke the other's language. The poor Indian was frightened and fearful through his pain and suffering that the worst was about to befall him, some terrible torture perhaps. In a moment of sublime enlightenment, the surgeon whispered in the dying man's ear, the name of the famous Indian mystic and poet, 'Rabindranath Tagore … Rabindranath Tagore'. Closing his tired eyes and with a serene and understanding smile, the Indian soldier understood and gave himself into the capable hands of the only person who could save his life. How I wonder can we learn to whisper 'Rabindranath Tagore' when we wish to communicate our most deeply-felt thoughts and ideas? From where can we find such inspiration in the depths of our being? Another example was in a church in the Cotswolds where a millennium stone had been set in the wall and beautifully carved to recognise a thousand years of worship in that place. A comment in the visitors' book was: 'I enjoyed looking round your Church and forgive me being pedantic, but are there not two n's in millennium?' Sure enough, on looking at the great black stone, it could be seen the mason had chiselled in only one 'n' and so the stone will probably remain for another thousand years. Stone masons do not have the advantage of spell checkers and delete buttons. But an 'n' or two does not really make much difference to the impact that such a place of reflection has had on generations of those looking to their inner lives over the centuries. Which is why I asked you to wonder about the millennium. I think that domes and wheels are all very well and I understand that not everyone will want to be in a place of worship of one of the great scriptural religions at that time. I wonder, though, whether anyone has given any thought, as they did in Berlin when the Wall came down, of men and women joining hands at that time around London or along the border between the Republic of Ireland and the Northern Province or around some part of the towns and villages in which they live.

While you continue to reflect on the millennium and the three circles of your life and how we can better communicate our thoughts, our feelings and our intuition, may I put into context the work I am doing with middle and senior managers and explain how I came to do this work.

My experiences over the last twenty-five years have convinced me that there is a growing and unfulfilled demand from many people in key positions of influence in the world to reflect on and perhaps be guided on their personal development and search for an inner path. Of course there are millions of others who may be in the same position, but I want to talk today about managers. Harry Bohan suggests that our conference this week addresses such subjects as: a vision for the next millennium; the human search for meaning; and managing the future. 'Are we forgetting something?' he asks. By organising this impressive conference he clearly has a mission, a mission which many of us share, and he sees the need to reach out to wider audiences. If it is a mission, if some of you feel it is your mission, then we must first work with and help those who are in a position to influence and help others – with teachers and politicians, with officials and managers in the public and private sector and opinion formers everywhere. I do not know whether it is your mission or even mine, but certainly there is a drumbeat within and beyond the walls of this conference. Although it may be muffled, many are beginning to march to its rhythm.

You will notice that my use of words is not very exact, that I have not defined what I mean by personal development or the inner self. I am just an ordinary person, like many of those I work with and if I am going to continue to work in this way, then I must remain an ordinary person. I once asked an eminent and extraordinary person what I should do to further my education in these matters.

'What books should I read?' I asked him. He advised me to study less with my head and feel more with my heart and that, as regards reading, 'Go to a library and let the books come off the shelves.' A few weeks later, I noticed among the many books around my home a few which I had read which might be relevant to my search and which I had forgotten. *Memories, Dreams and Reflections* by Carl Jung, *The Prophet* by Kahlil Gibran, Emerson's *Essays,* and *Travels with a Donkey* by Robert Louis Stephenson, as well as philosophy books from my university days and past careers which had scattered themselves around and which now, for the first time, I gathered together. There were in fact over thirty which I brought together. I saw that I had been searching over many years to discover my inner self. These books which came off my shelf confirmed my intention to see how I could work with managers to look at some of the issues which I had wanted to look at in my own life, but had not found a way. I had not been given permission to do so in the busy life which I and others lead on what I call the external or first path which we tread on our sparrow's flight from the cradle to the grave. The second or inner path branches off it somewhere along the way and is discovered by some people at some time in their lives. Many managers I believe are looking for this second path, the turning to which is often concealed by foliage which our busy outward lives help to proliferate.

But to begin at the beginning. Nearly twenty years ago I was a director at a famous European business school, responsible for the development of middle and senior managers who, after their three months of residential study, would return to their organisations in the public and private sectors and expect to achieve promotion to the higher echelons. They would be leaders of major companies within a decade. We taught them the usual aspects of management: finance and accounting, marketing and strategy, production and organisational behaviour, as human resource development was called in those days – both equally questionable terms, but it must be remembered that we are trying to get concepts across and perhaps words like these are children of their times.

Apart from this formal studying, we did different things. I took those managers walking in the mountains of the lake district where we worked on practical team problems in the open air. We visited companies in different countries – France, Belgium and Germany – to understand the different, especially cultural ways of doing business. We met officials of the European Union in Brussels and reflected on the future of Europe. We went jogging every morning in a beautiful park and listened to a doctor who talked about health and stress. Thanks to a wise and thoughtful Indian friend, we also, with some reservations, taught a few people to meditate. At the end of one three-month programme, a participant said that he thought these non-academic activities were as important as the rest of the course put together and another said that meditation had changed her life.

I reflected on these comments over many years and began to realise that what we were providing at the business school was space for participants to reflect not only on their business, but on the totality of their lives. Now with the advantage of hindsight, I can see how many managers were seeking to clear the foliage which was blocking their view of the second or inner path which I have described. That foliage was perhaps the relentless pressure under which they were being put to achieve organisational success.

It was only in recent years when, after a career in international business and government, I came back into a business school and academic environment to teach personal development as well as European Business on courses at the University of Durham Business School. We developed an approach which I would like to share with you. I started rather cautiously because we were not sure how managers would react. During the last part of my lecture today, I would like to share with you how the approach is working, what experience has taught us and what the problems are, but before that, in this second part, may I give you a taste of how I lecture to managers and what I say?

Would you therefore now imagine yourself (and if you are one already it will be easy!) to be a senior manager in a public or private enterprise sent to a business school to improve your management skills.

How can you manage the future? Where and with whom will you celebrate the millennium? What will you celebrate? How would you describe an ideal day in your life in the year 2000? Given a magic wand, what changes would you make now in your business, social and personal life? If we define clearly what we want, there is a better chance of obtaining it!

Not even Chancellor Kohl forecast the fall of the Berlin Wall and the uniting of the two Germanys. The subsequent collapse of communism was as unforeseeable as is much of our future on this planet. We can be certain though that during the next ten years rapid and dramatic changes will occur in western civilisation – changes much more condensed in their speed and impact than at any other watershed in history.

After hundreds of thousands of years as hunter-gatherers in a civilisation whose structure was tribal, we spent only three thousand years in an agrarian civilisation whose society was feudal. The Industrial Revolution saw the development of the nation state and an industrial civilisation which lasted for only a few hundred years. Now we find ourselves hurtling, in a few decades and at an ever-increasing pace, into an information, communications and technology based civilisation. Our society is becoming global, yet, paradoxically, individuals seek freedom to develop their private and personal agendas unimpeded by the restricting laws, rules and customs of the past. The nature of this new civilisation is global and individual at the same time.

There is thus a two-way pulling of our national roots – in one direction by steps towards world regional and global government – and in the other by the demands of local communities and individuals for greater freedom of action. This is exemplified for the UK by the drive on the one hand for further European integration and on the other by demands for more autonomy for the regions.

Just as our economic and societal arrangements are changing, so are we developing rapidly as individuals. We demand freedom which also means choice. Since the earliest times, we have discovered our gods in animals, trees and rivers and our beliefs in the mysteries of the universe and the shadow side of our souls.

Over the last two thousand years, the great organised religions with their scriptural traditions – Judaic, Christian, Islamic – have proclaimed universal and eternal truths. They largely replaced the village gods of antiquity. During the Enlightenment of the eighteenth century, developments in the natural sciences, the growth of historical understanding, and the widespread acceptance of critical thinking led to a gradual and partial revision of traditional religious attitudes. The effect has been to erode the influence of some traditional religions, leading to individual disappointment, disenchantment and dispossession. We are now witnessing the vacuum which this has brought about in the lives of individuals. It is being filled, however tentatively, by the rebirth of a personal, sometimes spiritual dimension in our lives. It is seemingly random and uncoordinated at this stage, but could lead to individuals attempting to better organise, direct and take responsibility for their own personal management and inner development.

In this period of change we are confronted by issues in the economic, social and personal spheres, which we see as three distinct parts of our lives:

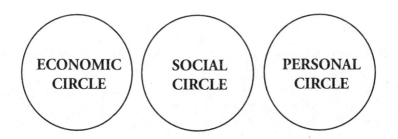

We are also experiencing different levels of a hierarchy of change. There is the day-to-day change to which we respond at a tactical level and a second level which concerns strategic matters. The third level I call the 'where has my business gone?' level, at which organisations, institutions, systems and industries dissolve into the past without very much warning. The fourth and fifth levels are even more dramatic, involving profound changes in the external environment and even in our civilisation. These last levels are unforeseen, sometimes unknowable and probably impossible to manage or forecast.

How can we as individuals and managers respond to these challenges? We cannot just walk away from them.

My personal view is that we should try to understand better the nature of change, to have some effect on the unfolding of events though studying the past, understanding the present and seeking a framework to discuss the future. We need to widen and deepen the debate and to thicken the thin veneer of the managerial stratum which Jung described as being:

> … fairly intelligent, mentally stable, moral and moderately competent – but do not overestimate its thickness…

Perhaps we can work on closer integration of our economic, social and personal spheres so that they look more like this:

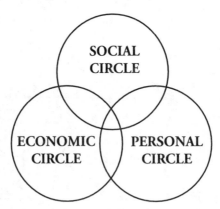

Understanding change, widening the debate and thickening the veneer would go some way to managing that part of the future we can influence. Rather like the tennis player awaiting a serve, we must train to be on our toes. The future is careering towards us like the serve coming over the net. We do not know at what speed it will be delivered or, whether, with top or back spin it will swerve left or right. But being aware and keeping ourselves mentally on our toes would give us a better chance of managing change. Saint-Exupéry wrote in *The Wisdom of the Sands:* 'As for the future, your task is not to foresee, but to enable it.' We could usefully reflect on our contribution to this process.

Conclusions

In this third part, I want to explain what follows on from the lecture I have just given you. In the first place I have been gratified to find how many managers accept the three circles approach and agree that their companies must look to their further integration. Some companies are well down this route already and others say that although they agree in principle, how does such an approach affect the bottom right-hand corner – their profitability. Others say that it will affect it even more adversely if they do not take it seriously now.

I offer managers on longer courses two follow-up lectures. The first is by a charismatic figure who tells the story of his or her life. In the second I draw attention to the key things that he has mentioned and show how the cardinal virtues seem to play a bigger role in his story than marketing and finance, planning and production which seem to be more or less mechanical activities once the issues of creativity, innovation, moral responsibility and concern for people as individuals have been properly resolved. I draw attention to a number of aids for personal development – a life-planning exercise, a decision-making formula, a visualisation approach, a stress reduction programme and, as part of that, a few sessions of meditation for busy managers.

There is an opportunity to meet with me and colleagues on a one-to-one basis and talk through issues to do with the programme, the workplace, their future. Conversations are open-ended. The experience of running these programmes has convinced me of a growing need for personal development and space for individuals to reflect on the totality of their lives. To assist in this could well be a new and developing role for business schools and perhaps university departments also, which would be more to do with facilitating than teaching, more with mentoring than advising. This will need new skills and new people. We are feeling our way cautiously in these areas but I think we may be reaching a sea change as we move towards the next century which, as that great thinker André Malraux said, will be spiritual or it will not be.

Tolstoy suggested that all philosophy and life could be reduced to two statements – 'how to live and what to live for'. It may be that we, in the materially richer countries or those developing that way, are beginning to understand the 'how to live' aspects which leaves the 'what to live for' part uppermost in our minds.

Ask yourself whether you are a hermit or a prophet. My view is that there is probably a hermit and prophet in many of us. We are on the continuum between the two, perhaps, both in our lives along the first or external path and along the second or internal path. We can reconcile the two roles as we can reconcile the two paths by accepting that they are not mutually exclusive, but complementary. We can if we wish be on a bridge or on many bridges between the two. When there is less activity on one of the two paths we can concentrate on the other: when we need to think – or feel – we can be hermits; when there are rivers to be forded or mountains to climb and new paths to discover, we can be prophets and help others and teach others on our way. Hermits and prophets, we are equally pilgrims and it is with the concept of being pilgrims that I should end.

The city of Samarkand may not be such a great place of pilgrimage as Rome or Jerusalem or Santiago de Compostela, but the essence of pilgrimages is to travel hopefully rather than to arrive. 'El strada es meior al il camino' – 'the road is better than the inn' as Cervantes puts it, although I prefer Stephenson who ends:

It is better to travel hopefully than to arrive and the true success is to labour.

But it was Samarkand which was remembered immortally in the poem by James Flecker and sums up for me what our role might be.

> We are the Pilgrims, Master, and shall go
> Always a little further. It may be
> Beyond that last blue mountain barred with snow.
> Across that angry or that glimmering sea
> White on a throne or guarded in a cave
> There lives a prophet who can understand
> Why we were born but surely we are brave
> Who take the Golden Road to Samarkand

Perhaps those of us privileged to understand that there are three circles and that they intersect, and who have discovered two paths and that they are complementary, can go always a little further. As hermits we go into our deeper selves, as prophets we spread some of the love and joy and insights we have been fortunate to discover along the way, and as pilgrims we joyfully unite the three roles as we seek as managers to unite the three circles.

A VIEW FROM THE CHAIR

John Quinn

The view was rather daunting – four hundred eager morning faces, bright and expectant at the prospect of an interesting line-up of speakers. Video-camera, lights, ACTION! Marie Martin hands over the Chair with graciousness and charm.

Our theme for the day is 'People and Place'. I draw down a topical reference from an obituary on poet Ted Hughes who died on Thursday – 'Place Maketh the Man'. So I hope today's deliberations will raise the questions. How important is it that people belong to place? Maintaining the poetry theme, I toss out a poetry quiz on the day's theme. The audience does well on Francis Ledwidge, poorly on Dylan Thomas and abysmally on Rupert Brooke...

Enter our first speaker, who (genuinely) needs no introduction. Professor Joe Lee – *sans* notes/script as usual and (horrors!) almost *sans* voice due to a throat infection, but as ever he rises to the occasion! The traditional Ireland from whence we got our sense of place is either dead or dying, we are told. Think traditional Ireland, think De Valera – and Joe Lee proceeds to decode De Valera's 'dream speech' of 1943 and suggests that it is still an ideal worth striving for.

'When I look back at the struggle we have had, I rejoice in the Celtic Tiger', the Professor argues. The downside of the Tiger is our fault – our failure to manage the multinationals has made us a prisoner of them. Joe Lee's argument swings to education – we now have the longest-educated young population we ever had, but is it the best-educated population? The RTCs, for example, were the best thing that ever happened to Irish education – in what they do and where they do it – but the danger lies in education leaning too much towards industrial needs to the detriment of the social side. Professor Lee asks some hard questions – have we ever really moved into being a liberal society? National wealth has increased 50 per cent in six years – what are we doing with it?

Let's find (positively) Irish solutions to Irish problems, he suggests, and he highlights in particular the need to link the generations, otherwise 'we have no society, we have no sense of place…'.

There is a buzz through the room as Joe Lee sits down. It's a good start to the day. One of the points he has made is that the 'pulpit' in the new order of authority sits in the corner of the living-room… . Cue the media man, Tom McGurk, whose brief is to look at the role and function of the media in the new millennium. He paints a grim (Grimm?) scenario. We are well down the route of tabloidisation, into the era of the sound bite, where image is all… . We are facing into an extraordinary society in the coming millennium – a society ravaged by consumerism and the new media age where the ratings rule and 'infotainment' wages war on journalistic standards. The *Sunday Business Post* man is unrelenting: 'Where is the sovereignty of fact?' Grim and grimmer. Yet all is not dark. 'The control is in your hands', we are told, 'because you elect those who regulate control'.

A lively discussion follows. Too lively, when I have to overrule people who insist on making statements rather than ask questions …Nevertheless, important questions are raised:

- In the matter of consumerism, are we the oppressors or the oppressed?
- Is too much expected of our schools?
- Why is history being downgraded in our curricula?…

It's time, thankfully, for lunch…

2.30 p.m. Enter David McWilliams, economist – young, dynamic, brash almost to the point of arrogance. The title of his presentation should have prepared us – 'From Boom to Bust and

Back' – but the man who allegedly coined the phrase 'Celtic Tiger' takes us on a breathtaking roller-coaster of lessons from history. Why some economies boomed, why others failed...

- Why was Mexico richer than the US in 1700?
- Why did Holland decline then re-emerge?
- Why did some tigers become tortoises?
- What are the lessons of history for us?

This young man is electrifying his audience. I am anxiously watching the clock but I know I will be devoured by that audience if I stop him now.

Can we avoid the crash? Maybe – if we introduce a property tax, tighten bank lending, use our common sense – BUT come it will with negative equity, rising emigration, possible bank failures, budget deficit by 2001 AD....

The message may be grim (is this the second of the Grimm brothers?) but the presentation is so professional, so honest and so wideranging the audience can only applaud loudly and at length. Did someone say Coffee? Yes, please. Strong and black.

And so to the final paper of the day. 'Is it possible to manage the future?' Now *there's* a question... . After all the scenarios the others have painted, this guy had better have an answer! 'This guy' is John Drew, a softspoken professor from Durham who highlights the need to turn to the inner dimensions of our lives. Suddenly we are back where we began yesterday, with Sr Thérèse recommending that we look into our inner selves. 'We need to integrate our personal, social and economic lives', John Drew tells us. He quotes Saint-Exupéry – 'we enable the future rather than foresee it' – and Malraux – 'The twenty-first century will be spiritual or it will not be....' The day is ending on a quiet, reflective note. We can be hermits and we can be prophets too. And we can also be pilgrims... .

There has been so much to absorb in this amazing day. The

questions at the end, ranging all over the place, perhaps illustrate this well.

What have I personally taken from it? (apart from abuse from the floor by a minority who felt I ignored them?)
A few points…

There are dangerous times ahead but we need not fear them if we ADAPT and EMBRACE CHANGE…

So much of what was said has implications for EDUCATION, a balanced, holistic education

We can be PROPHETS and PILGRIMS…

So maybe it wasn't such a scary day after all? But then… I pick up the newspaper in an attempt to relax after an exhausting day. Only then do I notice the date… 31 October… it's HALLOWEEN!

REFLECTION

I Hear An Army Charging

I hear an army charging upon the land,
And the thunder of horses plunging, foam about
    their knees:
Arrogant, in black armour, behind them stand,
Disdaining the reins, with fluttering whips, the
    charioteers.

They cry unto the night their battle-name:
I moan in sleep when I hear afar their whirling
    laughter.
They cleave the gloom of dreams, a binding
    flame,
Clanging, clanging upon the heart as upon an
    anvil.

They come shaking in triumph their long, green
    hair:
They come out of the sea and run shouting by
    the shore.
My heart, have you no wisdom thus to despair?
My love, my love, my love, why have you left
    me alone?

James Joyce

Part Three
Experience of Authority –
Authority of Experience

8

ONE WORLD – READY OR NOT

David Begg

It was originally suggested to me that I should make the title of my paper, 'Storming the Corporate and Institutional Bastille'. I declined this suggestion because I wanted to locate my contribution to this important conference in a more international context, reflecting the work in which Concern is engaged and seeking to relate that to our Irish experience of civil society. Another consideration, though, is that I cannot fairly represent myself as having a proven track record of successfully storming many corporate or institutional Bastilles.

However, I will address the subject of reform of the corporate and institutional sector in the context of globalisation of the world economy. I will seek to persuade you that the shift in the balance of power towards these sectors caused by the globalisation phenomenon makes the existing order of control and governance non-viable in the longer term. I will argue that nation states, even as their powers diminish *vis-à-vis* transnational corporations, must act to ensure that the governance structures of these bodies serve social interests and not just those of shareholders as happens in the existing corporate/financial nexus.

I will further argue that the vibrancy of civil society, by which I mean the means by which ordinary people act collectively to influence the quality of life, is a critical factor in this, and what happens in Irish civil society has an influence in the wider world. I have chosen the alternative title for the paper, 'One World – Ready or Not', to reflect my concern that the economic forces of globalisation are proceeding rapidly, while we have yet to get a handle on the social implications, in a world which, to start with, is very badly divided between rich and poor.

Notwithstanding what I said earlier, I can claim one very small modest success at storming the corporate and institutional Bastille. In 1991, I was the General Secretary of the Communications Workers Union and I was confronted with a very serious challenge. The Post Office, in which I represented the staff, was in poor financial circumstances and decided, with Government approval, on a radical plan to close rural post offices, install roadside letterboxes and, through various other means, get rid of two thousand postal workers.

The traditional reaction to this type of swingeing cutback would have been an industrial dispute, which would have been lost, because it would have alienated public opinion and this, combined with strong Government support, would have carried the day for the Post Office authorities. Instead we decided to mount a public campaign against the plan, making common cause with community groups throughout the length and breath of the country. To make a long story short, the plan was eventually withdrawn when political support for it collapsed in the face of Government back-benchers feeling the heat on the ground. Beyond this one experience, I was never more than a pimple on the backside of institutional or corporate authority in Ireland.

However, it taught me a great deal about the complex nature of civil society in Ireland. The campaign involved seventy public meetings, which were very well attended. I remember one night in Killarney, overhearing two elderly gentlemen discussing the meeting. One said to the other, 'What are two farmers doing at a union meeting? I can't stick those fellows'. The other replied, 'Neither can I, but if these post boxes come in everybody will be rooting in them to see how much is in the creamery cheque!'

The point is, our democracy is about more than electing a government. It is about different interests in society combining to hold that government accountable, even though the same interests may be in tension with one another for much of the time. It is the totality of these relationships that makes up civil society. Whenever I travel to Asia or Africa I realise just how fortunate we are to live in a society, which I admit is far from perfect, but which contains so many checks and balances on authority. I would like now to explore what Irish civil society can offer the world at large.

The world is a wondrous place, filled with gorgeous, striving, capable people, who are endlessly interesting in their differences and likenesses. Still, it is true, neither technological invention nor economic revolution has yet managed to eliminate folly and error from the human condition.

Forty years ago John Kenneth Galbraith wrote *The Affluent Society*. The central argument in the book was, that in the economically advanced countries, there has been a highly uneven rate of social development. This year the United Nations Development Plan (UNDP) asked him to write a piece for its annual Human Development Report, exploring the latter-day relevance of *The Affluent Society*. In the course of his contribution he made this observation:

> Were I writing this now, I would give emphasis to the depressing difference in well-being between the affluent world and the less fortunate countries – mainly the post-colonial world… . The problem is not economics. It goes back to a far deeper part of human nature. As people become fortunate in their personal well-being and as countries become similarly fortunate, there is a common tendency to ignore the poor or to develop some rationalisation for the good fortune of the fortunate. Responsibility is assigned to the poor themselves. Given their personal disposition and moral tone, they are meant to be poor. Poverty is both inevitable and, in some measure, deserved. The fortunate individuals and fortunate countries enjoy their well-being without the burden of conscience, without a troublesome sense of responsibility. This is something I did not recognise,

writing forty years ago; it is a habit of mind to which I would now attribute major responsibility.

In addition to these changes mentioned by Galbraith, one could perhaps identify two other major changes, particular to the last ten years. The first is the virtual collapse, or certainly considerable debilitation, of two great value systems, Christianity and Marxism. The second is the phenomenon known as globalisation. Globalisation represents the comprehensive victory of capitalism over communism, but it is unfortunate for all of us that the diminution of social values has left us bereft of a global ethic with which to harness and control the forces of inequality released by this new economic order.

Globalisation in the twentieth century is a process of global economic integration, broadly driven by market forces, in particular, the competitive price pressures to reduce costs, but the actual events of industrial movements depend crucially upon political transactions – irregular deals that often offend the reigning principles of free-market enterprise. When a multinational corporation seeks to shift production to low wage labour markets, a process of political bargaining ensues, with governments competing for new factories. Concessions are offered, deals are made, investment follows.

In this environment, commerce is able to leap across the deepest social and economic divisions, bringing advanced production systems to primitive economies, disturbing ancient cultures with startling elements of modernity. Governments of developing nations may be nervous about the cultural disruption, but they usually suppress doubts and dissent.

We in Ireland have benefited hugely from globalisation, but even successful nations discover that a basic insecurity lingers in the economic advance. A prosperity based on the strategies of multinational corporations remains a hostage to them. If a country manages to graduate from low wage status and establish a self-sustaining industrial base, its achievements may become permanent, but the very process of moving up also threatens to drive away the global investors. If capital does eventually move on, a relationship, intended to be a mutually rewarding symbiosis, may prove to have been parasitic.

Global integration of the consumer market also has a social dimension. With the breakdown of national boundaries in trade, communications and travel, people all over the world are becoming part of an integrated consumer market – with the same products and advertisements. The most obvious example of this is McDonalds. Worldwide sales expanded by $19 billion between 1986 and 1996 – 64 per cent outside the United States.

But integration has been an uneven process – making many products available for a few but visible to many. While the global elite are consumers in an integrated market, many others are marginalised out of the global consumption network.

The stark reality is that our planet is a very unjust and unequal place.

- New estimates show that the world's 225 richest people have a combined wealth of $1 trillion, equal to the annual income of the poorest 47 per cent of the world's people (2.5billion).

The enormity of the wealth of the ultra-rich is in mind-boggling contrast with low incomes in the developing world.

- The three richest people have assets that exceed the combined GDP of the forty-eight least developed countries.
- The fifteen richest have assets that exceed the total GDP of Sub-Saharan Africa.
- The wealth of the thirty-two richest people exceeds the total GDP of South Asia.
- The assets of the eighty-four richest exceed the GDP of China, the most populous country, with 1.2 billion inhabitants.

Another striking contrast is the wealth of the 225 people, compared with what is needed to achieve universal access to basic social services for all. It is estimated that the additional cost of achieving and maintaining universal access to basic education for all, basic health care for all, reproductive health care for all women, adequate food for all and safer water and sanitation for all is roughly $40 billion a year. This is less than 4 per cent of the combined wealth of the 225 richest people in the world.

Let us turn now to look at the role of the international institutions and governments in the global market. The recent Asian crisis does not inspire confidence. *The Financial Times,* in an analysis piece on 7 September 1998, opined:

> A growing worry is, that as the legitimacy of governments is threatened by their inability to overcome the recession, they will resort more freely to nationalism and find it harder to control the forces they unleash.

The World Bank has admitted that the dramatic increase in private investment in developing countries has been thrown sharply into reverse. By mid-1998 there was an alarming decline of 25 per cent and within the last month there has been 'a much more dramatic gap'. The Bank reckons that as many as twenty million people have been thrown into poverty in Indonesia and Thailand alone. In a separate report, the International Labour Office says that since the global crisis started, worldwide employment has climbed by ten million to 150 million. In addition, 25 to 30 per cent of the world's three billion labour-force are underemployed – with all the social exclusion that entails.

It is of significance that these developments have occurred against the background of a weak framework of prudential oversight in banking. East Asian economies had poor regulatory and supervisory arrangements in the financial sector, and weak corporate governance and financial disclosure requirements. Nor has the effect been confined to Asia. Market-driven tightening in global financial market conditions, indirectly required a $35 billion bail-out of the large US hedge fund, Long Term Capital Management (LTCM), in September.

In terms of the forces at work, there are some key differences between the present situation and previous periods of instability in the world economy. In particular, the interaction between private sector behaviour, institutional structures and financial liberalisation has not been experienced before.

Tony Blair and Bill Clinton have spoken a number of times recently about their mutual desire to find a 'Third Way' between the socialist command economy model and unregulated free market capitalism. William Hague ridiculed this notion at the Tory Party conference, saying that there was no such thing as a 'Third Way' – only 'A British Way'.

The Sun, in an exceptional feat of intellectual prose, labelled Hague and the Tory Party as a 'Deceased Parrot' for his pains. For once *The Sun* may have been right!

The problem with Blair and Clinton's rhetoric about the 'Third Way', is that so far it has not gone beyond rhetoric. For what it's worth, my view is that governments must seek to enforce a new model of global corporate governance in addition to reform of the institutions controlling the financial system.

The responsibility to change from shareholder-driven corporate governance to one which includes much wider goals is primarily one for the governments of the major trading nations.

To reform the financial system (which is essential) and leave the issue of corporate governance for another day would be a major mistake.

The history of industrial development has taught societies everywhere to think of the economic order as a ladder. Some people are high up on the ladder. Others are struggling to climb it. The new dynamic of globalisation paints a different metaphor in people's minds – a see-saw – in which some people fall in order that others may rise.

Neither the ladder nor the see-saw is a satisfying metaphor, since both excite explosive resentments and rivalries. Neither promises to lead to a global system that is both prosperous and stable, equitable and tolerant, since both rely inherently on exploiting the inequalities among peoples and societies. The political temptation to interrupt the globalising process – to stop the erosion by somehow smashing the system – is sure to grow stronger in the advanced economies because the losses are growing larger. The spate of factory closures in the north-east of England in the last month is an example.

The only way out of this dilemma is to think anew, to reject the choice between one side and the other. The political values known as human rights are not marginal matters reserved for idealistic reformers. These issues are integral to how the global economy functions and how it imposes consequences on wage earners everywhere, in rich nations as well as poor. In crude terms, the top of the ladder will continue to fall if the bottom is not brought up more rapidly. Bringing the bottom up would be very difficult to achieve in the best circumstances. It is impossible to imagine as long as people at the bottom lack the political freedom to demand it.

For the first time in human history, though most people don't yet grasp it, a fateful connection is emerging between the first and the last. One end of the ladder (or see-saw) cannot defend its own general prosperity without attending to human conditions at the other end. For masses of people in the global marketplace, economic self-interest is converging with altruism.

Understanding this new reality will be very difficult for people, especially in the richest nations, especially among business and political leaders, since it suggests a very different conception of the national interest. In order to escape the dilemma, people have to re-imagine an economic order based on different metaphors. Not a ladder or a see-saw. Perhaps a vast playground where many different children are playing together and separately, but all playing the same game.

When I was involved in the campaign to save rural post offices one of my strongest supporters was T. J. Maher, who was then an MEP. I always had great admiration for T.J. and for his ability, as leader of the IFA, to bring every subject, somehow or other, back to farming. I must try to emulate him by relating the subject of this paper to the work of Concern. Frankly, I rarely have the opportunity of addressing a distinguished audience so I cannot let the opportunity pass.

To the question, 'Who is my neighbour?', the Bible answers that Christ responded with the parable of the Good Samaritan. Whether people contribute to the work of international aid agencies from a Christian or secular humanitarian motive, this depiction of someone who acts immediately and without qualification to relieve the urgent physical suffering of another person, is a powerful one. But in today's world the reality of the conditions in which we operate is more complex.

What should the good Samaritan do if he travels the same route every day for several years, and finds another victim of the muggers each week at the roadside? Treat each victim with the same kindness? Give up his acts of compassion on the grounds that his purse will not bear the demands? Or begin to ask what is wrong with this particular road, or the society through which it passes?

What should he do if he arrives on the scene, one day, in time to witness the muggers in action? Wait until they have gone and help the victim? Attack the muggers and compromise the purity of his response, or indeed risk injury himself? Or raise the matter in another place?

What should he do if he discovers that one of the muggers is a member of the family of the victim? Or that the muggers are working a protection racket in the area? Or that they are hoods acting to collect rents on behalf of an extortionate landlord? Or that they work on behalf of a cartel of grain merchants who seize the produce of the poor, paying a fraudulently low price, and including those who protest? Or that the victim is not ailing from a physical beating but from having food taken from him or denied him?

Dilemmas of this nature, affecting human rights, are confronted every day in many of the countries in which Concern works. We see extra-judicial killings, abuse of refugees by host governments, suppression of political opposition and corrupt and inadequate judicial systems. These conditions do not just exist in the rogue countries but often in countries considered democratic and heavily supported financially by western governments. The consequences of an operational agency like Concern confronting these abuses are potentially serious. We risk our operations being closed down and our expatriate staff being expelled. For our national staff the consequences may be even worse.

Notwithstanding these difficulties, it is the overriding mission for Concern and our sister agencies to seek to build civil society in the countries in which we work. Without human rights there cannot be a functioning civil society and so human rights considerations must inform everything we do. The fact that there are difficulties does not mean we can say that the position is hopeless and we must concentrate on a simple humanitarian agenda. The position is not hopeless. The fostering of strong human rights cultures by the governments of South Africa, Botswana, Malawi and Namibia show how wrong it is to condemn the rest of the Developing World to lower expectations.

This, then, is the link between the nature of our own society, here in Ireland and what we work to create in the Developing World. Galbraith, in the article I quoted earlier, also observed that 'Nothing is so important for economic development and the human condition as stable, reliable, competent and honest government'. At a macro level, governments in the Developed World can best use aid transfers to achieve democracy, an independent judiciary and a free press. But good governance also requires political accountability and the matrix of social organisations, which demand it on the part of the people. That is what Concern does in its development programmes. It helps people to organise themselves to take control of their own destiny by building their capacity.

This work can best be done from a platform which itself is based in civil society in this country. In this way we give to our work the legitimacy and the authority of experience based on the active overseas involvement of men and women from every walk of life. Therefore, the quality of our work will depend on the quality of our own civil society and the values which influence it.

This conference has identified a theme upon which many people today are focusing in the privacy of their own lives. What are we about?, Where exactly is the rapid pace of change leading us?, Are we forgetting something? I read somewhere recently that the German-born management guru, Drucker, offered the view that politics were becoming less and less relevant – that large-scale organisational and business change in this century has happened without political consequences. This is too simplistic. It ignores, for example, the conditions which facilitated the rise of Fascism in his own country.

I contend that Drucker is wrong. I suggest that there is a continuum between politics in its most basic form, that is, in the way people engage in civil society, and the governance institutions and corporations in the new world order, and whether this new world order is to be inclusive or to serve the consumer élite of the Developed World only.

In so far as this conference provides a forum in which people can reflect on where the rapid pace of change is leading us it does a public service. There is no doubt that many people today are confused and unhappy; even though we live in the midst of material wealth, most of us over forty never dreamed of in our youth. The Pope has just issued an encyclical on it.

Reflection is good, but so is action. Some years ago there was a song written by Ralph McTell which contained the words, '*So how can you tell me you're lonely, and for you the sun don't shine? Let me take me you by the hand and lead you through the streets of London, and I will show you something to make you change your mind*'. Whatever about the streets of London I could certainly show people of this disposition streets in Addis Ababa, Dakar, Maputo and Port Au Prince that would change their perspective.

I will conclude by paraphrasing Karl Marx when he said that philosophers merely interpret the world, the secret is to change it. If anybody here would like to help to to change the world, Concern can offer you the opportunity to make a difference. It is a non-denominational membership organisation with a democratic structure. There are many ways in which you can support our work – without having to go abroad – although people with suitable qualifications willing to work overseas would be most welcome just now. If you think you might be interested give us a call.

9

SOCIAL ENTREPRENEURSHIP – A NEW AUTHORITY?

Mary Redmond

The anthropologist Margaret Mead said 'If you look closely you will see that almost anything that embodies our deepest commitment to the way human lives should be lived and cared for depends on some form – often many forms – of volunteerism'.

My law practice is rooted in the 'World of Work' so I begin my topic from home territory. Its obituary – Work I mean – is written every day of the week. The main culprit for the projected demise of Work is 'the computer'.

Arthur Schlesinger Jnr, US historian and former adviser to President John Kennedy, put it dramatically:

> The computer turns the untrammelled market into a global juggernaut crashing across frontiers, enfeebling national powers of taxation and regulation, undercutting national management of interest rates and exchange rates, widening disparities of wealth both within and between nations, dragging down labour standards, degrading the environment, denying nations the shaping of their own economic destiny, accountable to no-one, creating a world economy, without a world policy. Where is democracy now?

In the information society, the society of the new millennium, jobs are changed rapidly, as the European Commission in its Green Paper *Living and Working in the Information Society, People First* (1996), reminds us. There is a decline in continuous full-time working and a corresponding surge in atypical work and self-employment.

Yet from the beginning our civilisation has been structured more or less around the concept of work. This applied to the hunter gatherer, to the farmer, to the medieval craftsman, to the line worker in the factory this century. Work as we know it is being systematically eliminated. A recent book, *The Corrosion of Character, the Personal Consequences of Work in the New Capitalism,* by Richard Sennett suggests that it is time to take a sober look at the way we work. There have been radical changes in the course of the recent economic boom. Perhaps one of the most persistent is 'no long-term' – the concept of employability. Sennett argues that the flexible work ethic undermines self-discipline and does employees real social and personal damage.

The European Commission in its paper attempts to stimulate public debate around its concern, amongst other things, that the information society will produce great divisions between the digitally élite and their opposite numbers.

Because the importance of formal work in our lives is diminishing, because of the increasing dependencies of poverty and disadvantage in our society, an alternative vision must be found.

During this conference we have heard about what we may be forgetting in the society of the new millennium. We have heard of the importance of catering for spiritual as well as economic needs in Ireland's current economic success, and that we must work towards partnerships of different kinds, between 'ordinary people', voluntary organisations, corporations, and the State. 'Europe must search for a soul as a matter of urgency.'

It is social entrepreneurs, I believe, who will provide the alternative vision that is needed to complement the information society. In the community and voluntary sector ('the voluntary sector') soul is alive and feeling. By 'soul' I mean moral or emotional or intellectual life, spirituality.

Voluntarism brings forth an energy or intensity in the community which is emotional and intellectual. It is driven by the vast energy that makes up human life all around us. To those in the voluntary sector value in life is not solely the attaining of some aim through creating something of material value. The 'meaning of life' is not a question one can devote much time to – instead the social entrepreneur thinks of herself as being questioned by life, daily. For the social entrepreneur the answer consists not in talk and research and position papers but in right action and in right conduct. In a conviction that if we want to hear more of the good rather than of the bad we must take responsibility for it. We must do it ourselves. Some unidentified 'they' will not do it for us. Nor is 'their' permission needed to take action.

What are social entrepreneurs? Not all who are involved in voluntary work are social entrepreneurs. They are harbingers of change, people in innovative voluntary organisations who devise new ways to provide support and development for those excluded from the opportunities of the information society.

They identify under-utilised resources – people, buildings and equipment. Their output is social: they promote health, welfare and well-being. Their core assets are forms of social capital – relationships, networks, trust and co-operation. In turn this gives access to physical (e.g. rundown buildings) and to financial (fundraising, donations, corporate giving) capital. The social entrepreneur needs to find the right human capital. Eventually the work begins to pay dividends. The organisation is social in the sense that it is not owned by shareholders and does not pursue profit as its main objective.

Innovativeness and vision are essential. The stakeholders are the community, the beneficiaries, staff, volunteers, and investors/partners.

Above all, the activity is not for profit. It is the activity of the gift economy. The gift of a person, him or herself, their time, their talents, their energies. When we give of ourselves we truly give. Khalil Gibran said:

There are those who give little of the much which they have – and they give it for recognition... . And there are those who have little and give it all. These are the believers in life ... . There are those who give with joy, and that joy is their reward. And there are those who give with pain, and that pain is their baptism. And there are those who give and know not pain in giving, nor do they seek joy, nor give with mindfulness of virtue... . (*The Prophet*)

Giving in the voluntary sector likewise has many mansions. Some give from a cup, others from a surging river. Voluntary organisations, public corporations and the private sector intersect like three large circles. Where they intersect in common segments you will find entrepreneurs.

There is a lot happening at the moment. A White Paper on supporting voluntary activity is imminent. The idea of a community trust is under active study, and this will involve the public and private sector together supporting voluntary activity. These initiatives stem from the State.

I don't think we are forgetting the voluntary sector, therefore, but can it be called a new authority as the title of my paper asks?

Potentially, yes. As yet, no.

There is something missing in the voluntary sector. It is the gelling of its energy into a powerful countervailing view of 'the voluntary sector', capable of many things, including influencing and, even, setting the agenda for this nation.

The notion has surfaced before. It is not new. It has generally been received with little enthusiasm because it belongs to the category of 'impossible to do'.

Recall that the vision of technological utopians, that people would go and machines come in their place, was unattainable just a hundred years ago. When the time is right, things happen.

We all agree that the time is right to supplement (not supplant) the values of the market-place which have predominated to date.

The social entrepreneur is not yet the new authority because at present voluntarism is dotted all around the margins of public and private life. In places voluntarism is strong, in others it is weak. It is organised, it is disorganised. It is big, it is small. It is well resourced, it is under-resourced. It – all of it – needs to be brought to the centre.

Politics is the 'art of the possible' as Lord Butler said. What is being suggested here is political, but not in a party political way. Understanding and bringing leadership (action) to bear on the implications of the Information Age is an imperative. A leader is someone who doesn't like to go anywhere by herself, and I am happy to say that mine is not a lone voice.

There are others who would attempt 'the art of the possible', try to make something more cohesive out of the voluntary sector, and with their permission I shall name them : Fr Sean Healy, Sr Brigid Reynolds, Sr Stanislaus Kennedy, Fr Peter Mc Verry, Sr Bernadette McMahon, Sr Phyllis Lee, Sr Eileen Foley, Sr Mairead Kelly, Sr Bridget Callaghan, Ms Kay Conroy, Ms Mary Paula Walsh, Ms Carole Shubotham, Mr Brendan Collins, Mr Denis MacNamara and Mr Alan Mitchell. We have met a few times and as we continue to meet we want more and more to join us.

My paper is about a voice – as yet unheard as 'new authority' – that of the voluntary sector.

The wheel of voluntarism is yet unturned. Think of how powerful it will be when it is turning, its spokes accommodating the rich diversity of the voluntary sector, its centre the distillation of the great energy which drives it.

The origin of these meetings started for me when I addressed the Dublin Chamber of Commerce on the social entrepreneur last year. What I said was later synopsised in a Sunday newspaper. The response to what was published showed I was pressing a green button.

I was looking over my experience of several years in the Hospice Movement, trying to work out why 1 had been put out, made intuitively uncomfortable, by the word 'charity'. It was the image of cap in hand, the provoking of pity, the 'spontaneous giving' of 'charity' that discomfited me. You cannot imagine groups who evoke pity coming together to form an identity.

I hoped to create alliances between the voluntary and corporate sectors by bringing about a paradigm shift in corporate perceptions of voluntary organisations. I wanted companies to become pro-active in the pursuit of social goals by identifying and entering into partnership arrangements with socially entrepreneurial partners. What I overlooked was the fragmentation of the voluntary sector. Partnership when it comes between the three sectors must be at arm's length, between parties sharing burdens and benefits together. An unequal or fragmented partnership can not be really effective. Before alliances and partnerships can take place in a fruitful way, the voluntary sector needs to find its proper place.

In response to what was published I heard from people in many walks of life, who saw in the voluntary sector a vital antidote to materialism, as well as a vital prescription for the post-market era. Most lamented the sector's lack of cohesion. All were united in their passion for voluntarism. They are right, of course.

Ireland's 'Voluntary Sector Directory' (if it existed) would make compelling reading. While market and government sectors are often credited with advances in our society, the voluntary sector has played an essential part in creating our schools. hospitals. hospices, social service and health organisations, clubs, youth organisations, justice and peace groups, conservation and environmental groups, animal welfare organisations language groups, theatres, orchestras, art galleries, libraries, museums, community development and enterprise schemes, neighbourhood alert systems, and so on. There are thousands of voluntary groups all over the country. What powerful social glue.

Consider what a coming together of the voluntary experience could yield to our society:

- The incubation of new ideas and forums to air social grievances (including 'how work can screw you up').
- The integration and inclusion of persons who would otherwise be excluded.
- The provision of a helping hand to the poor and helpless.
- The preservation of good traditions and values.
- New kinds of intellectual experiences.
- Practice in the art of democratic participation.
- Friendship.
- Time and space to explore the spiritual dimension of our lives.
- Experience of the pleasures of life and nature.

The structure of the wheel of voluntarism will not be hierarchical. The voluntary sector can not be trapped or tamed. Those of us who have met so far agree, above all, that all will break bread equally in the new identity. We see equality between groups, big and small, as vital. We see other values too, such as autonomy, diversity and the friendship of networking.

A key word is change. Coming together will mean personal transformation together with community and environmental change. Voluntary groups themselves will benefit from greater cohesiveness, from being in the strongest position to look for and get the 'building bricks' for an infrastructure, for voluntarism, in our legal, tax and education systems, for example. 'Lobbying' will be a different experience. Education and development will benefit everyone involved.

One of my favourite stories is recounted in Cicely Saunders' *Beyond All Pain*. It relates to a patient in a hospice, Enid Hencke, who literally had to fight her way to peace. She found her profound dependence hard to bear. She gradually accepted the reality of what was happening and found the answer which she dictated the month before she died.

A friend and I were considering life and its purpose. I said, 'Even with increasing paralysis and loss of speech, I believe there was a purpose for my life... . I was then sure that my present purpose is simply to receive other people's prayers and kindness and to link together all those who are lovingly concerned about me, many of whom are unknown to one another'. After a while my friend said, 'It must be hard to be the wounded now, when, by nature, you would rather be the good Samaritan'.

It is hard: it would be unbearable were it not for my belief that the wounded man and the Samaritan are inseparable. It was the helplessness of the one that brought out the best in the other and linked them together... . If as my friend suggested, I am cast in the role of the wounded man, I am not unmindful of the modern day counterparts of the Priest and Levite, but I am overwhelmed by the kindness of so many 'Samaritans'. There are those who, like you, have been praying for me for a long time and constantly reassure me of continued interest and support. There are many others who have come into my life – people I would never have met had I not been in need, who are now being asked to take care of me. I like to think that all of us have been linked together for a purpose which will prove a means of blessing to us all.

That story illustrates so well the interconnectedness which is a theme of this conference. In this case between those who are involved in voluntary work, those they care for, the wider community around them. There is but one world in which we will work out our salvation. *Orare est laborare. Orare* is not a part-time responsibility.

As we straddle the new millennium we have freedom of choice. We can influence the direction in which we go. The information society offers wondrous possibilities for creative change. Let finding the proper place and role for the voluntary sector be one of them.

A VIEW FROM THE CHAIR

Michael Kenny

Our experience of authority might lead us to believe that the influence of the corporate sector, through globalisation, could undermine democratic society. However, David Begg, drawing on his experience of the wider world, comforted us in the realisation that there is a more optimistic vision for society, especially where civil society is vibrant. Mr Begg pointed out that a vibrant civil society can hold the state accountable for its action, can ensure that the poor are not ignored as affluence increases and that altruism can be fostered. Mr Begg suggested that where civil society is vibrant and informed, a model of society as a vibrant playground could prevail. In this playground the strong, i.e. the corporate, the affluent, the institutions and the state, interact at all levels with all other sections of society in multifaceted ways, resulting in a better society. He said that in the new millennium the parable 'Who is my neighbour?' will be more complex but could be more effective.

Dr Mary Redmond highlighted the same divisions in society, but suggested that while the digitally élite are prospering in modern Ireland, and confidence in the market and politics is declining, there is tremendous soul and spirit in the voluntary sector. Dr Redmond suggested that in the new millennium social entrepreneurs will bring change, will innovate and will find new ways and means of supporting those needing support in health, welfare and general well-being. This will be achieved through a new partnership of the private and the voluntary sector. In this way the voluntary sector have more in common with the private sector than they realise. This commonality of vibrancy and focus on need will become more evident as society seeks new ways of supporting the poor in the new millennium.

However, Dr Redmond warned, the voluntary sector (made up of approximately 7,250 voluntary organisations) is very fragmented and needs to consolidate to partner the private sector equally. If that happens then the voluntary sector can provide the 'social glue' that will enable the private sector to complement the state and deliver more effective service through the voluntary sector.

David Begg suggests that future partnership action plans, involving the private, state and voluntary sectors, to address inequality and poverty should be grounded in principles of human rights. Both speakers demonstrated that there is adequate experience within the voluntary sector, at home and in the wider world, to competently partner the state and the private sector for a better society in the new millennium that means we will not 'forget' something important. It is exactly that experience that will be the new authority for the new millennium. David Begg further suggested that this authority of experience can have a valuable influence on the wider world.

REFLECTION
An Irish Blessing

May the blessing of light be with you –
light outside and light within
May sunlight shine upon you and warm your heart
'til it glows like a great peat fire
so that the stranger may come and warm himself by it.
May a blessed light shine out of your two eyes
like a candle set in two windows of a house,
bidding the wanderer to come in out of the storm.
May you ever give a kindly greeting to those whom you pass as
you go along the roads.
May the blessing of rain – the sweet, soft rain –
fall upon you
so that little flowers may spring up to shed their
sweetness in the air.
May the blessings of the earth – the good, rich earth –
be with you.
May the earth be soft under you when you rest upon it,
tired at the end of the day.
May earth rest easy over you when at last you lie under it.
May earth rest so lightly over you that your spirit
may be out from under it quickly,
and up, and off,
and on its way to God.

Traditional Irish

LIST OF CONTRIBUTORS

Sr Thérèse, Abbess of the Poor Clare Convent, Ennis, was born in Scotland of Irish parents. She grew up in northern Rhodesia/Zambia. Educated by the Notre Dame sisters in South Africa, she worked in Barclays Bank before coming to join the Poor Clare Sisters in Ennis in 1961. She believes passionately in the contemplative life and in its irreplaceable contribution to our world. The Poor Clare charisma includes the contemplative stance, a deep care for creation, and peace.

Mark Patrick Hederman has been a monk of Glenstal Abbey in Limerick for over thirty years. A former headmaster of the school, he did his doctorate in the philosophy of education. He has lectured in philosophy and literature in America and Nigeria as well as Ireland, and was a founding editor of the cultural journal *The Crane Bag*. He studied philosophy in Paris with Emmanuel Levinas and is interested in art as a prophetic pointer towards a more comprehensive and humane future for all of us.

John Lonergan, Governor of Mountjoy Prison, was born in Co. Tipperary in 1947, and is married with two teenage daughters. He joined the Prison Service at Limerick in 1968 and in 1984 he was appointed Governor of Mountjoy Prison in Dublin. He became Governor of Portlaoise Prison in 1988, but returned to Mountjoy in 1992. Mountjoy is Ireland's largest prison accommodating over 750 men and 60 women. He has frequently underlined the fact that large numbers of our country's youth are at risk in today's society. He stresses that these young people believe that the Celtic Tiger is out of their reach.

Marie Martin, formerly a teacher of modern languages, is the European/International Officer with the Western Education and Library Board in Northern Ireland. She has a responsibility for promoting European and international school links and projects. She has made a specialist study of the spirituality of French writers of the early twentieth century and is also interested in the ecumenical movement and in the role of the laity in the Church. She has a particular interest in Celtic spirituality, in its relevance to our time and in its potential for nourishing the human spirit in the new millennium.

Professor Joe Lee is the Head of the Department of History at University College, Cork. He has at various times been an Administrative Officer in the Department of Finance, Dublin, a Fellow of Porterhouse, Cambridge, and an Eisenhower Fellow. He has held Visiting Appointments in several European and American universities, and was an independent member of Seanad Eireann on the National University of Ireland panel. His book, *Ireland 1912-1985*, was awarded an Aer Lingus/*Irish Times* prize as well as the Donnelly Prize of the American Conference for Irish Studies.

Tom McGurk, columnist and writer with *The Sunday Business Post*, distinguished broadcaster, writer and journalist, has worked widely in Ireland and Britain as a presenter with RTÉ, Thames, Granada and BBC Radio 4. His extensive list of television documentaries include: *Aunt Annie's Bomb Factory* (ITV) – which reopened the Maguire and Guilford bombing cases; *From Gorby With Love* (Channel 4); *Stolen Children – Argentina's Dirtiest War* (ITV) – an international award-winner. His latest documentary, *Long Journey Home* (Disney/PBS), the history of Irish America, which took over four years to make, was broadcast by RTÉ in July/August. He spent four years as a Foreign Correspondent with *The Mail On Sunday* and currently writes a column for *The Sunday Business Post*. His screenplays include *Dear Sarah, Emperor of Ice-cream* and *The Need to Know*. He is a Jacob's Award winner for both television and radio documentaries.

David McWilliams is Senior Economist and Strategist at Banque Nationale de Paris (BNP) Emerging Markets Group, London. The group invests in almost all central and eastern European markets, particularly Russia and the Balkans. In addition, BNP trades in a variety of other eclectic emerging markets from North Korea to the Ivory Coast, and from Cuba to Algeria. Prior to joining BNP, he was Senior Economist in the Union Bank of Switzerland from 1994-1997. In a previous life, David McWilliams was a Central Bank Economist in Dublin, and kicked off his career at the European Commission. He was educated at Trinity College and The College of Europe.

John Drew MA, AM, MBA, Hon FIL, is a Director of the New Cross Disciplinary Research Institute for the Study of Change at Durham University and Visiting Professor of European Business Management at Durham University Business School. He is president of the Institute of Linguists, Director of The Change Group International Plc and consults on European Business and Executive Development. He was the UK representative of the European Commission from 1987 to 1993. He has worked in business, government and academia on aspects of European integration. Formerly First Secretary in the UK Diplomatic Service, he was subsequently Director of Marketing and Executive Programmes at the London Business School, Director of International Corporate Affairs at Rank Xerox and Director of European Affairs at Touche Ross International.

John Quinn is a senior producer with RTÉ Radio 1, since 1977. His programmes have won numerous distinctions, including three Jacobs Awards, and International Awards in Japan and New York. He has specialised in educational series and in documentaries. His weekly educational magazine *The Open Mind* is now in its tenth year. Born in Ballivor, Co. Meath, he was educated at Patrician College, Ballyfin, Co. Laois and St Patrick's College of Education, Dublin. A former teacher at both primary and post-primary levels, he is a recognised editor in educational publishing. He has written five novels, four of them for children, one of which won a Bisto Children's Book of the Year Award, and he has edited two best-selling editions of his radio interviews – *A Portrait of an Artist as a Young Girl* and *My Education.*

David Begg is Chief Executive Officer of Concern, Worldwide, an agency engaged in relief and development activities in eighteen countries throughout the Developing World. He joined the ESB in 1971 as a technologist, having qualified in electrical engineering practice at Kevin Street College of Technology. In 1979 he became a full-time trade union official and was appointed General Secretary of the Communications Workers Union in 1985. He was elected to the Executive Council of the Irish Congress of Trade Unions in 1986 and served on that body until 1997. During this period he was involved in the negotiation of the National Partnership Agreements between government, employers, workers and farmers. From 1995 to 1997 he was Vice President of the European Organisation of the Postal, Telephone and Telegraph International. He became a Director of the Central Bank in 1995. He left the trade union movement to take up his present position on the retirement of Fr Aengus Finucane in July 1997.

Dr Mary Redmond is a solicitor who runs her own practice specialising in Employment Law, and is on the Board of the Labour Relations Commission. She is founder of the Irish Hospice Foundation, of which she is now Patron. She is a Director of the Bank of Ireland Group and of Jefferson Smurfit Plc and has previously been a member of the Equality Employment Agency and of the Higher Education Authority. Since 1996 she has been Professor (Adjunct) at the National College of Industrial Relations and she is also a member of the Institute of Directors of Ireland and Fellow of the Royal Society of Arts. Prior to 1985 when she set up her own practice, she was involved in academic life at University College, Dublin and, before that, Churchill College. She is an honorary member of the Senior Common Room at Somerville College, Oxford. Her doctorate from Cambridge is on Termination of Employment. She has written several books on Employment Law and one on Constitutional Law. Her second edition of *Dismissal Law* is about to be published.

Michael Kenny is a lecturer in rural and community development at the Centre for Adult and Community Education, St Patrick's College, Maynooth, Co. Kildare. Mr Kenny has worked in local development since 1980, with the exception of over five years spent in rural and community projects in central and east Africa. He is active in a number of local and overseas development projects in which he works to develop participatory development and community practice.